Walt Disney's
MAGIC KINGDOM
Disneyland U.S.A.
ANAHEIM, CALIFORNIA

To all who come to this happy place...
WELCOME.

Disneyland is your land. Here age relives fond memories
of the past... and here youth may savor the challenge and
promise of the future.

Disneyland is dedicated to the ideals, the dreams, and the
hard facts that have created America... with the hope
that it will be a source of joy and inspiration to all the
world.

LEGEND
- ★ RIDES & ATTRACTIONS
- ◎ FUTURE DEVELOPMENTS
- ⑧ RESTROOMS
- ☎ TELEPHONES
- ✚ FIRST AID
- POLICE (LOST & FOUND)

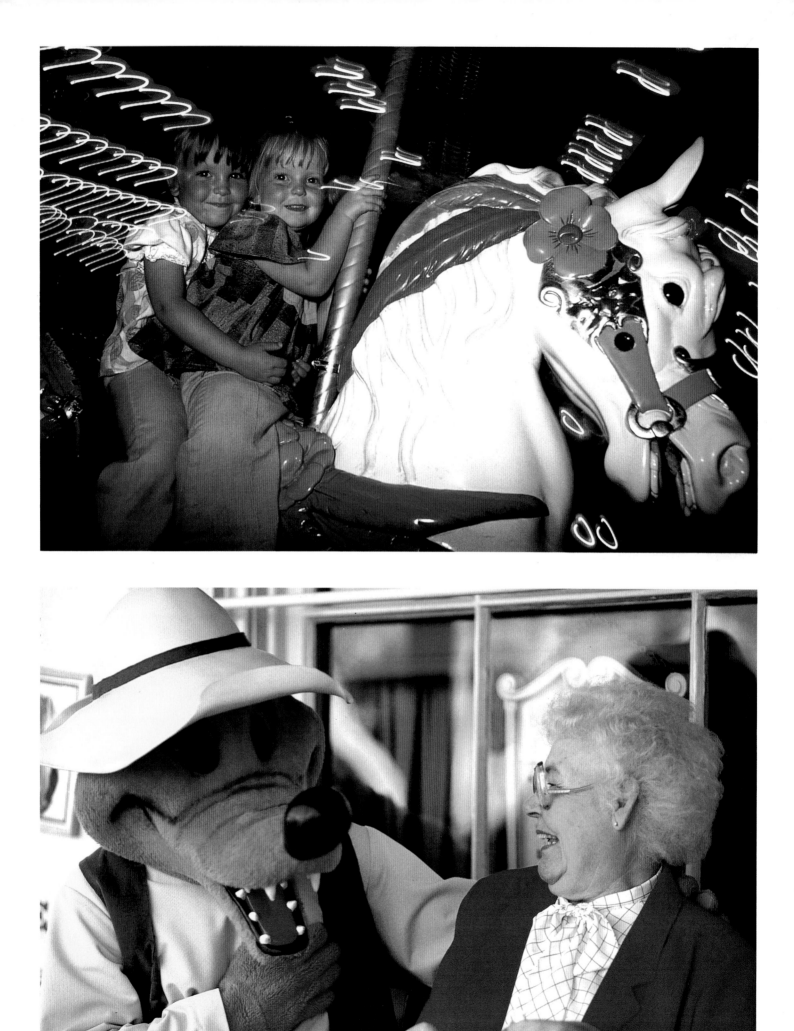

DISNE

Y L A N D

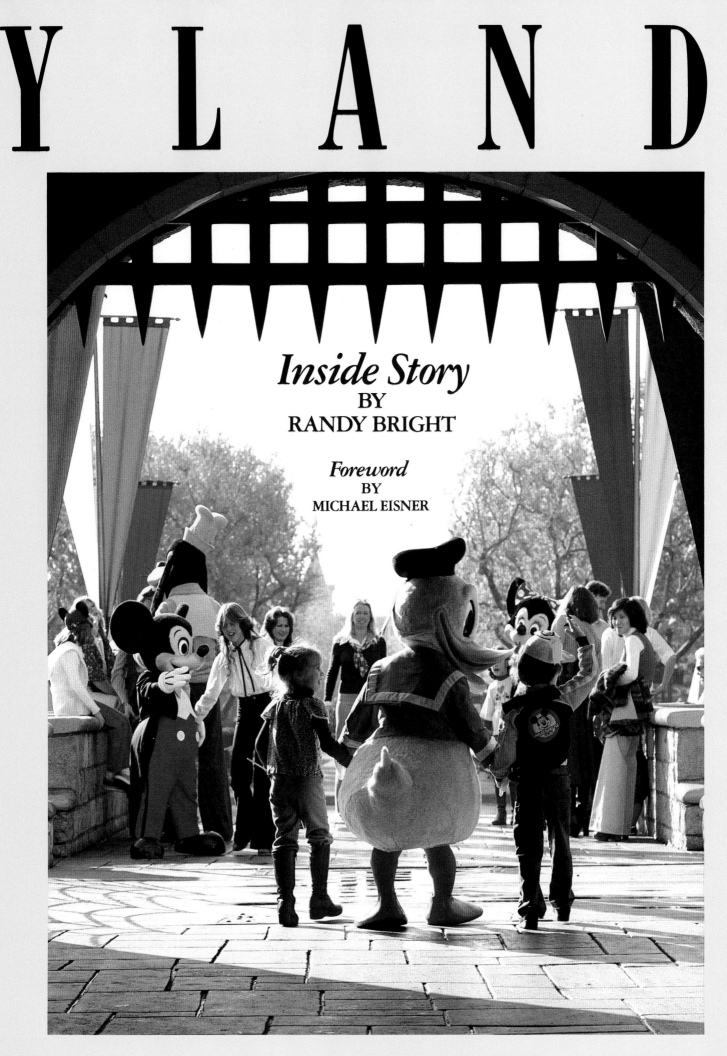

Inside Story
BY
RANDY BRIGHT

Foreword
BY
MICHAEL EISNER

HARRY N. ABRAMS, INC., PUBLISHERS, NEW YORK

DEDICATION

*To Mark, Wendy, and especially to Pat, the
pretty, blue-eyed, blonde Disneyland tour guide
whom I met "at sea" on the* Columbia *sailing
ship and shanghaied to be my wife.*

Page 1: *The* Mark Twain *steams along Frontierland's Rivers of
America.*

Pages 2–14: A *"day in the life" of the Magic Kingdom begins
with early morning deliveries (above, left). The traditional
dropping of the rope signals a mad charge down Main Street,
U.S.A., as young visitors sprint to their favorite attractions
(right). Less hurried guests take the leisurely Horse-Drawn
Street Car (below, left). Pages 4–5: Sleeping Beauty Castle,
with Matterhorn Mountain rising in the background, provides
the gateway to Fantasyland. Pages 6–7: The day's visit might
include a spin on the King Arthur Carrousel (above, left); a
close encounter with a Disney character (below, left); lunch
in the shadows of a Bavarian-inspired castle (right). Pages 8–9:
It might involve an adventure with Big Thunder Falls in Davy
Crockett Explorer Canoes. Pages 10–11: And it might mean
returning home with a special friend (left) and special memories
(right). Right: Big Thunder Mountain Railroad provides the
fastest transportation on the frontier Page 14: A day in Disneyland often ends with the sparkling Main Street Electrical
Parade (left).*

Page 15: *The Country Bears celebrate Christmas in Bear Country.*

Project Director: Darlene Geis

Editor: Lory Frankel

Designer: Dirk Luykx

Page 181: "It's a Small World." Words and Music by Richard M. Sherman
and Robert B. Sherman © 1963 Wonderland Music Co., Inc.

Library of Congress Cataloging-in-Publication Data
    Disneyland: inside story.

    1. Disneyland (Calif.)—History. I. Title.
    GV1853.3.C22A525   1987   791'.06'879496   87–1767
    ISBN 0-8109-0811-5

Times Mirror Books

Printed and bound in Japan

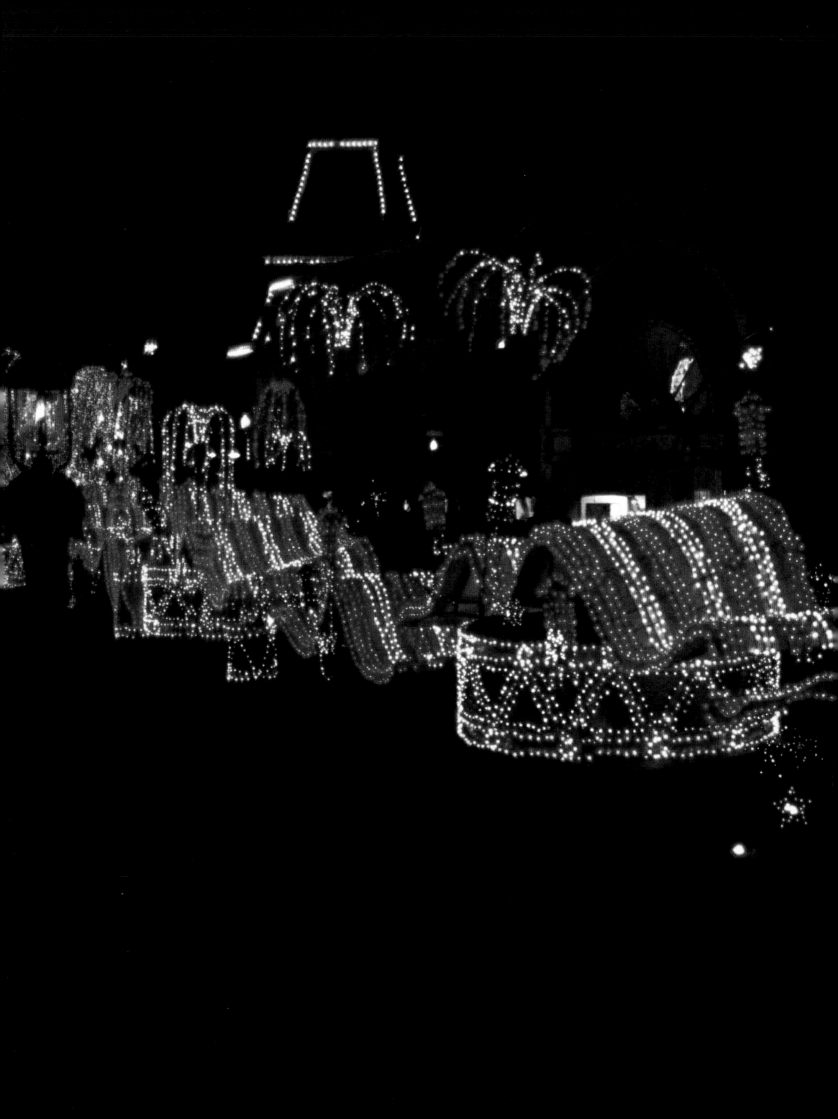

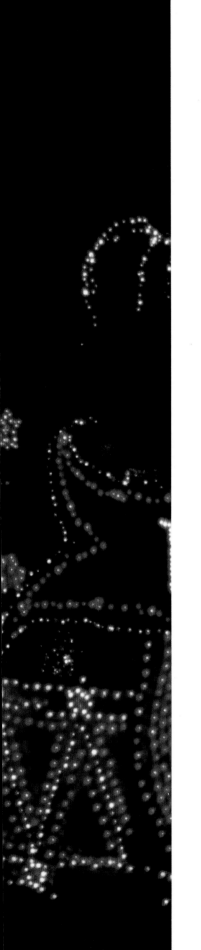

Contents

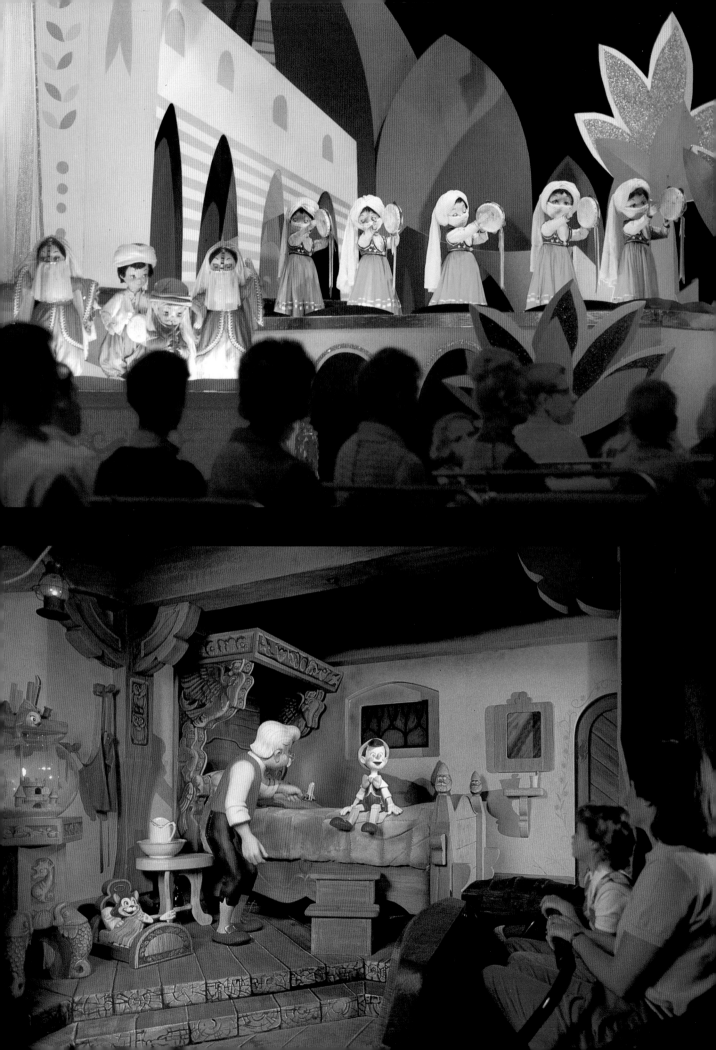

Foreword

Like most youngsters in the post—World War II years, I grew up watching Mickey and Donald and Brer Fox and "The Wonderful World of Disney."

But Disneyland was an impossible dream. In those days, thirteen-year-old New York kids didn't travel cross-country to live out their fantasies, not even in the world's greatest theme park.

Years later, as tourists, my wife Jane and I finally entered the gates of the Magic Kingdom. Whatever youthful images I'd once conjured up were dwarfed by the beauty and spectacle of the place. The reality was better than the illusion.

That was almost twenty years ago. Sad to say, I'm no longer often able to look at Disneyland through the eyes of a visitor. The park that once was solely my pleasure is now part of my job.

Today there are other, newer Disney parks—in Florida, in Japan, and, soon, in France—but Disneyland remains our flagship. Everything we've built since 1955 is a reflection of its creative spirit. Most of our best new ideas still get their start in the original Magic Kingdom.

On that first, long-ago visit, Jane and I stepped from the chill and gloom of an Eastern winter into the sunny glow of Main Street, a place so clean that it seemed we could eat right off the sidewalk, a place where our cares and concerns somehow couldn't get past the gate.

In these pages, Randy Bright helps me recapture those first-time feelings. I'm sure this book will rekindle gentle memories in everyone who has entered Disneyland's world of warmth and wonder.

Michael Eisner
Chairman, The Walt Disney Company

Colorful Arabian dancers are among the large international cast of It's a Small World (opposite, above).

Geppetto finally gets a son on Pinocchio's Daring Journey (opposite, below).

Author's
Note

The summer of 1959 was a very special one for this writer. As a college undergraduate, I had enlisted in the Disneyland navy and was scheduled for active duty aboard the sailing ship *Columbia*, the newest vessel to ply Frontierland's Rivers of America.

We circumnavigated the Rivers of America time and again, and I marveled at the frontier wilderness that the Disney landscapers had created out of Anaheim's former orange groves. Only three years after the Park's opening, the sparsely planted forests had already rapidly filled in the barren spots. It was easy to suspend disbelief here and pretend I was on a real sailing ship in 1787, probing the mouth of the real Columbia River.

The evening shift was even more captivating. I have never in my life had so moving an experience as when we would drop anchor at the far turn of the river to see the "Fantasy in the Sky" fireworks show. With all the wonder of a small child, I watched through the ship's rigging as the colorful skyrockets exploded high above in the summer sky. I wasn't in Anaheim, California, at all. I was in some faraway place, not unlike the make-believe world of another child of Disney—Peter Pan. And I was being paid for the fantasy.

Sometime later, I was fitted into a silver metallic suit, adorned with a radio-equipped belt and other paraphernalia that couldn't be identified. With one last touch, a clear helmet was placed over my head, and two oxygen tanks were strapped to my back. I was ready to venture into the final frontier. I was now the Disneyland Spaceman.

More than twenty-five years have passed since I first roamed Tomorrowland as an earthbound astronaut. But today I am still privileged to be able to try new things, working with the extraordinary staff of Walt Disney Imagineering. In many ways, *Disneyland: Inside Story* is their story, because it is the story of Imagineering, the powerful combination of creative ideas and the technological know-how that brings them to reality. Long secluded and kept in low profile, the Imagineering think tank came into being as WED (an acronym for Walter Elias Disney), the company Walt Disney formed to create Disneyland. In December 1986, reporters from *U.S. News and World Report* toured the facility and immediately dubbed it "Hollywood's Best-Kept Secret." The following pages open the door a little wider into the near-reclusive world of Disney's Imagineers. It is through their talents that Disneyland continues to be a marvel of discovery and innovation more than three decades after Walt Disney first saw his dream become reality.

ACKNOWLEDGMENTS

No person can write the inside story of something so universally admired as Disneyland without heartfelt thanks to those who are truly inside Disney.

I remember Bo Boyd's first call, asking me if I knew someone who might be interested in developing this project. I immediately thought of two people who qualified as both writers and participants who had lived the Disneyland dream from its early years. One was my boss, Marty Sklar. The other was me. As fate and fortune would have it, Marty had already decided that I should be given the opportunity to write the story of Disneyland in this major publication. Thanks, boss.

Thank you also to Dave Smith and Paula Sigman, for their remarkable organizational abilities and dedication in ensuring the accuracy of the manuscript. The book could never have been completed without access to the Disney Archives. To Sherrie Rains, for keeping the Disney-Abrams communications channels wide open. To Pat Sellon, Joann Centeno, Jerry Schneider, and Ernie Bailey for helping to locate the best visuals to make this book something extraordinary. To Carl Bongirno for paving the way for my participation in bringing the project to publication. To John Hench and Tony Baxter, whose thoughts and feelings about the Disney philosophy span the past, present, and future and stand for all that we strive to create. To David Mumford, and, most of all, perhaps, to Bruce Gordon, for his good humor, perseverance, and ever-present help in keeping this author on track up to the book's successful completion. To Darlene Geis and Lory Frankel of Abrams for their patient assistance and to Dirk Luykx for his care in designing the best possible book.

A very special thanks to all those who are part of the Disneyland story for your own unique contributions, any one of which, I found, is a story in itself, symbolic of that which makes Disney so special in the minds of everyone.

Overlooking Disneyland, about 1976. At foreground, a floral Mickey Mouse in front of Main Street Station greets visitors as they enter.

Introduction

There was a time when residents of Southern California boasted that they could visit the mountains, desert, and seashore all in a single day's drive. Yesterday's optimism, however, has long since given way to the realities of traffic-snarled freeways lacing the sprawling megalopolis that is today's Los Angeles basin. The natives, however, can still lay claim to another boast. They can visit a thickly forested wilderness, a picturesque southwestern desert, a dense equatorial African jungle, a perfectly preserved turn-of-the-century town, a space center, a Caribbean village, and a European castle complete with its own mountain backdrop . . . all in a single day. And there's not a traffic-infested freeway in sight—getting around is half the fun, aboard horse-drawn trolleys, submarines, steamboats, bobsleds, canoes, teacups, river launches, rocket jets, pirate ships, monorails, and steam trains. In the middle of Southern California, a land wall-to-wall with shopping centers, condominiums, and parking lots, lies the oasis of fantasy known the world over as Disneyland.

THE INTERNATIONAL CELEBRITY

More than 270 million people from every walk of life and every country around the world have visited Disneyland since its gates opened on July 17, 1955. Perhaps even more astonishing than its popularity with the general public is the Park's consistent appeal to visiting dignitaries and celebrities. On any given day, guests may find themselves walking side by side with political leaders, entertainment and sports stars, major corporate executives, and almost every other category of national or international notable.

These distinguished visitors may arrive incognito or accompanied by special-security people or hostesses. Sometimes, though, they simply prefer to remain ordinary visitors, melting into the "Disneyscape" with friends and family. Rock superstar Michael Jackson, a Disneyland regular and one of the Magic Kingdom's greatest fans, does little to disguise his appearance during his visits (thereby burdening the Park's operating officials with the kind of crowd-control problems publicists only dream about). Filmmaker George Lucas of *Star Wars* fame readily admits to having grown up with the Park as his favorite playground.

"Old Dobbin," pulling the Horse-Drawn Street Car (above, right), competes with such newfangled horseless carriages as the Motorized Fire Truck (above, left) on Main Street, U.S.A.

Captain Hook's Pirate Ship (below) anchored in Skull Rock Cove until 1982, when a new Fantasyland was created.

For many years, graceful swans have made the Castle moat their home (above and below, right), *while other creatures have settled in Adventureland's African Veldt* (below, left).

President Dwight D. Eisenhower takes over as skipper on the Jungle Cruise.

American political leaders who have visited the Park include presidents Harry Truman (who would not ride Dumbo because of the Republican symbolism), Dwight D. Eisenhower (who may have ignored Frontierland's mules for a similar reason), John Kennedy, Richard Nixon, Jimmy Carter, and Ronald Reagan.

The Magic Kingdom has long been on the itineraries of foreign heads of state such as King Mohammed of Morocco, King Baudouin of Belgium, Prime Minister Muldoon of New Zealand, Emperor Hirohito of Japan, Anwar Sadat of the United Arab Republic, and many others. The list is so long that the *Christian Science Monitor* observed, with tongue only partly in cheek, that Disneyland had "almost become an instrumentality of American foreign policy."

A CRITICAL PERSPECTIVE

For all the accolades, Disneyland has not been without controversy. A few years after the Park's opening, Julian Halevy wrote in *The Nation* that

Clockwise from above, left: *India's Prime Minister Nehru, Senator Robert Kennedy and astronaut John Glenn, Crown Prince Akihito and Crown Princess Michiko of Japan, and entertainer Nat "King" Cole are among the many distinguished guests of Disneyland.*

The glitter of Main Street, U.S.A., fades to the tranquility of the hub, where all roads lead to adventure.

In Disneyland, even security hosts and wastebaskets are designed to blend with their surroundings. This one (above) is located at Fort Wilderness on Tom Sawyer Island. Similarly, the graphics for lost children areas are intended to minimize anxieties of "lost parents" (below).

In honor of the thirtieth anniversary of Disneyland in 1985, "The Gift Giver Extraordinaire" began giving gifts to every thirtieth guest to enter the Park.

Disneyland should be equated with Las Vegas. "Their huge profits and mush-rooming growth suggest that as conformity and adjustment become more rig-idly imposed on the American scene, the drift to fantasy will become a flight."

Others, such as science-fiction author Ray Bradbury, have been equally quick to defend Disneyland. "The world is full of people who steadfastly refuse to let go and enjoy themselves," replied Bradbury to Halevy's comments. "On my first visit, I accompanied one of the great theatrical and creative minds of our time, Charles Laughton. I've never had such a day full of zest and high good humor. Mr. Laughton is no easy mark; he has a gimlet eye and a search-ing mind. Yet he saw and I found, in Disneyland, vast reserves of imagination before untapped in our country. Disney makes mistakes, but what artist doesn't? But when he flies, he really flies. I have a sneaking suspicion after all is said and done that Mr. Halevy truly loved Disneyland, but is not man enough or child enough to admit it."

Equally effusive in his praise of Disneyland was the highly respected mas-ter planner and builder James W. Rouse, who said in his keynote speech be-fore the 1963 Urban Design Conference at Harvard University, "I hold a view that might be somewhat shocking to an audience as sophisticated as this—that the greatest piece of urban design in the United States today is Disney-land. If you think about Disneyland and think about its performance in relation to its purpose; its meaning to people—more than that, its meaning to the process of development—you will find it the outstanding piece of urban design in the United States. It took an area of activity—the amusement park—and lifted it to a standard so high in its performance, in its respect for people, that it really has become a brand-new thing. It fulfills all the functions it set out to accomplish unself-consciously, usefully, and profitably to its own-ers and developers. I find more to learn in the standards that have been set and in the goals that have been achieved in the development of Disneyland than in any other single piece of physical development in the country."

Disneyland. Is it pure escapism? Is it a playground for the child that lives within us, imprisoned in some, running nearly out of control in others? Is it merely a flight to an idyllic fantasy or possibly a study model for future envi-ronmental planning? People's perceptions of Disneyland vary widely and wild-ly, but no one can deny what Disneyland is not. It is not, as so many early detractors thought it would become, "a Hollywood spectacular—a spectacular failure." It is the ultimate manifestation of one man's dream begun more than a half-century ago—a simple dream for "a place where parents and children can have fun together."

CHAPTER ONE

The Elusive Dream

To all who come to this happy place: Welcome. Disneyland is your land. Here, age relives fond memories of the past, and here youth may savor the challenge and promise of the future. Disneyland is dedicated to the hard facts that have created America —with the hope that it will be a source of joy and inspiration to all the world.

DISNEYLAND DEDICATION PLAQUE, JULY 17, 1955

DISNEY, IWERKS, ISING, HARMAN (HUGH)

"Disneyland really began when my two daughters were very young," Walt Disney has said. "Saturday was always Daddy's Day, and I would take them to the merry-go-round and sit on a bench eating peanuts while they rode. And sitting there, alone, I felt that there should be something built, some kind of family park where parents and children could have fun together."

The carnivals, fairs, and amusement parks of the day were usually dirty, disorganized, and poorly run. Walt envisioned a whole new kind of park. It would be clean, safe, friendly, and, most important, it would give parents the opportunity to participate in the adventures with their children.

Walt Disney's dream of a family park may have been revolutionary in concept, but it was evolutionary in execution. From the inception of the dream in the late 1930s to its realization in 1955, it survived World War II, a near financial collapse of the Disney Studio, countless revisions of the idea, and the ever-present skepticism of critics who said it would never work.

Innovative, high-risk projects had been a hallmark of things Disney ever since Walt opened his first studio in 1922, producing silent animated shorts in Kansas City. The following year found him Hollywood-bound. With his brother Roy, who took care of business matters, he set up the Disney Studio in an inauspicious location, the rear of a real estate office just down the street from his uncle's home, where he lodged. It was a humble beginning, and the next few years saw success tempered by disappointment.

Then, in 1928, the new star arrived. He was almost called Mortimer, but Walt soon changed his name to Mickey, the main character of history's first talking cartoon, "Steamboat Willie." Mickey Mouse became not only a household name but an international star, and Walt Disney was finally on his way to a long and astonishingly innovative career in the world of show business.

He created the first full-color cartoon, "Flowers and Trees," and the first full-length cartoon feature, *Snow White and the Seven Dwarfs*. In *Fantasia*, he introduced audio depth through the first use of stereophonic sound. And he gave animation visual depth through the remarkable Multiplane camera, which photographed a scene as a composite of planes, each painted on a separate sheet of glass, creating a startling three-dimensional effect as the camera moved through the scene.

With the advent of World War II, Walt found his important overseas

The Carolwood-Pacific miniature steam engine makes a run through Walt's backyard in stylish Holmby Hills, California.

markets closed off, and the steady stream of income that paid for innovation dried up. The Studio, now located on a brand-new lot in Burbank, turned to producing training films for the military.

Even during the bleak war years, Walt never stopped dreaming of the next frontier. A Studio staff member recalled that Walt talked about possibly opening the Disney Studios to guided tours. The public increasingly expressed an interest in visiting the birthplace of Snow White, Pinocchio, and other Disney characters, and Walt was intrigued with the idea of showing off the Studio, even providing a train ride around the lot. But the idea lay dormant as the company continued to struggle through the early postwar years.

Disney's wife, Lillian, believed that it was Walt's longtime fascination with trains that really provided a focus for Disneyland. In 1948, Walt had gone down to the Studio machine shop seeking help to build a miniature HO-gauge model-railroad layout for his nephew's Christmas gift. He met Roger Broggie, who helped him assemble the system. (Broggie later became a key figure in the realization of Disneyland.) Broggie watched as Walt went about creating his HO miniature landscape with the same zeal he applied to the creation of his motion pictures. When the Christmas gift was completed, Disney then posed the next challenge: "Okay, this is a toy electric train. Now what's for real?" Soon they were looking into "live steam," the railroad buff's lingo for a real live-steam locomotive.

For Lillian Disney, "the real thing" would come to have a profound influence on where the Disney family lived. She and her daughter Diane had been looking for a suitable location for their new home. They found an excellent location near downtown Los Angeles, but it was too close to the hustle and bustle of Wilshire Boulevard for Walt's liking. And it had no room for his train.

A large piece of property in Holmby Hills proved just perfect for their new home—and, of course, for Walt's train.

Actually, Walt's train wasn't exactly "the real thing" either. It was, indeed, live steam, but not full size. It was, fortunately for his neighbors, only one-eighth scale. The model drawings were derived from a single photograph and a blueprint from Southern Pacific Railroad of locomotive #173, originally built in the late nineteenth century. Disney, with the aid of Broggie and others in the Studio machine shop, fashioned a perfect working miniature replica of the engine and immediately dubbed it the Lilly Belle, after his understanding wife. The project caught the attention of railroad enthusiasts around the country, who bought more than sixty duplicate sets of drawings

Disney's Lilly Belle captured the imagination of another generation.

and castings. The income from this little sideline paid for the entire cost of engineering and building the project.

The Lilly Belle provided enough live steam power to chug around 2,600 feet of track in the Disney backyard. Walt dubbed his new railroad the Carolwood-Pacific, after the location of his home, on Carolwood Avenue. It soon became a familiar, if not bizarre, sight to see Walt straddling the little locomotive and riding around his property like an overgrown boy riding an overgrown toy. Weekend parties at the Disneys' often included guests from the motion-picture industry, and it wasn't unusual for a well-known actor, producer, or studio head to take turns testing the train's thirty-mile-per-hour capability on the track's tight curves.

The operation of Walt's train was not without its problems, though. It jumped the tracks a number of times; once it turned completely over, knocking the safety valve off the engine and burning a child's leg with steam vapor. Walt was soon convinced that he needed Broggie and an assistant to keep the

In 1954, Walt poses next to old #173, the actual train that the Lilly Belle was modeled after.

An early concept sketch shows Main Street, U.S.A.

train running at his social gatherings. He could no longer play host, bartender, engineer, and fireman simultaneously. He also knew that whatever form his family park might take, a train would be a central part of the idea.

FROM KIDDIELAND TO AMERICANA

One of Disney's first thoughts was to build a small playground for kids on a corner of the Studio property, where they could have all the things he thought they ought to have but didn't at nearby Griffith Park. One of those things, naturally, would be his train.

It seems only fitting that when Disney met another future Disneyland contributor a short time later, in 1951, it would be in a model-train shop, in London. Walt had long admired Harper Goff's pictures of American scenes

published in *Esquire* and *Coronet* magazines. Over dinner that evening, he asked Goff to come to work for him. "But I don't do animation, Walt. I'm a live-action man," Harper exclaimed. Walt replied, "Well, you're doing story-boards at Warners, aren't you? I've got a little thing up my sleeve that I really want to do. It's sort of a 'Kiddieland,' and I want it to be called 'Walt Disney's America.' I don't want to just entertain kids with pony rides and slides and swings. I want them to learn something about their heritage." Disney went on to tell Goff how much he admired his magazine sketches of such subjects as Wilbur Wright, the Erie Canal, and other highlights of American history. Goff was soon at the Disney Studio, assigned to a private room off limits to other employees, with orders to keep the door closed.

Not far away from Goff's secret office, one of Disney's key animation storymen, Ken Anderson, was already working on another secret project. Walt had taken Anderson off the Studio payroll just after Ken had finished his work on *Lady and the Tramp*, and was paying him out of his own pocket to work on a traveling exhibit called "Disneylandia." "You guys can draw and paint and do things with your hands," Walt told him, "and you don't think I can. Well, I can draw and paint, too, you know. And I can build things. You and I will have this little room and the only keys to it. You can make some paintings like Norman Rockwell's, and I'll build models of them."

Anderson designed twenty-four scenes, each to be built in miniature by Walt. The grand idea was to create a series of elaborate stage sets with minia-ture characters that would animate after being activated with electric eyes. Earlier, Walt had returned from New Orleans with a mechanically animated bird. By pushing the technique further, he believed he could gain the technol-ogy to animate his little tableaux for "Disneylandia." He intended to bring American folklore and history to life in animated shows and present them to schoolchildren across the country.

The initial scene he tried to animate was the first one he built from Ken Anderson's sketches, a tap-dancing man in an old-fashioned theater environ-ment. He hired performer Buddy Ebsen to come in and dance in front of a grid pattern while being photographed. Analyzing the film frame by frame, Roger Broggie and Wathel Rogers, an affable mechanical wizard with strong anima-tion training, tried to reproduce Ebsen's movements in a one-eighth-scale me-chanical dancing figure, standing about nine inches high. The result was an intricate, if crude, entanglement of cables, cams, and ineffective controls. After many weeks of painstaking effort, an exasperated Broggie told Walt they were no further advanced than the seventeenth- and eighteenth-century kings

Disney directs Buddy Ebsen in the filming of a "Dancing Man" sequence. Animators later used it to program the movements of Walt's first three-dimensional animated character. This was the forerunner of the remarkable Audio-Animatronics *figures.*

of France who had commissioned the creation of little automatons that played musical instruments, including a complete orchestra in miniature that had been built for Louis XVI.

"If we could just go to some research and development on a full-size figure," Broggie said, "there are devices being developed in aircraft controls that may give us the upper hand." Although no one realized it, this was the beginning of what would one day evolve into Disney's stunning form of three-dimensional animation, *Audio-Animatronics*. For the time being, however,

Back in the early 1950s, Walt had an idea for a traveling exhibition of tableaux called "Disneylandia," for which this scene, "Granny's Cabin," was built. It was one of the many evolutionary steps that led to Disneyland.

Walt felt that the smaller figures would be more magical and unique. His miniature world began to expand considerably. Anderson had sketched a scene from Disney's motion picture *So Dear to My Heart*, affectionately known as "Granny's Cabin." Walt reproduced the set from Anderson's drawings, and he himself planned to build the figure of the grandmother in a rocking chair.

By this time, Harper Goff had plunged into the project full-time while Ken Anderson was off doing work on *Sleeping Beauty*, Disney's next animated feature. Goff designed a set for a barbershop quartet, perhaps the most ambitious of the miniatures, in which all four figures were to break into harmonious song. But once again, the diminutive scale hampered the possibilities for realistic animation.

Even had it proved successful, a cost analysis revealed that twenty scenes of similar scope, with people constantly putting quarters in every coin slot, would not take in enough money to pay for the maintenance. Disney finally came to the conclusion that he was going to have to build his miniature Disneylandia on a full-size basis and combine it with his Kiddieland park into one major project at a permanent location. The name of the project would be shortened from Disneylandia to the more familiar "Disneyland."

THE BURBANK PLAN

Harper Goff was assigned to lay out a basic plan for the new full-size Disneyland park, on sixteen undeveloped acres across the street from the Studio in Burbank. It was a perfect location, right next to the Los Angeles River. There would be "singing" waterfalls and fountains, pony rides, statues of the Disney characters, picnic areas, a roller-coaster ride that would go over a simulated broken bridge, and perhaps a museum display for Walt's beloved miniature American scenes. Best of all, of course, would be the live-steam train that would run along the river's edge straight into nearby Griffith Park. Most important, it would be clean and safe, without the "carny atmosphere" that plagued most parks of the time. It would be the culmination of Walt's dream of a family park, where parents and children could have fun together.

All these new ideas expanded the plans for Walt's Kiddieland park so dramatically that they made Roy Disney's original 1952 budget allocation of $10,000 for project development look woefully "underwhelming."

Undaunted, Goff and Disney took their preliminary plans and sketches to the Burbank City Council in order to solicit the city's support. Despite Walt's enthusiastic description of a family park, a councilman got up and exclaimed, "We don't want the carny atmosphere in Burbank. We don't want people falling in the river, or merry-go-rounds squawking all day long." Walt walked out. He had earlier heard a similar response from his wife, Lillian, when he first talked over the idea with her. "Why would you want to get involved with an amusement park?" she asked. "They're so dirty and not fun at all for grown-ups. Why would you want to get involved in a business like that?"

"That's exactly my point," Walt replied. "Mine isn't going to be that way. Mine's going to be a place that's clean, where the whole family can do things together."

Eventually, much of the land first selected for Disneyland would find another, totally unrelated, use. The Burbank tract became part of the Ventura Freeway, one of the main arteries of the expanding Southern California freeway system. It was just as well, anyway, because the plans and ideas had already far outgrown the sixteen acres across from the Studio.

THE GREAT LOCATION SCOUT

Quickly, and in deepest secrecy, the Disney staff began to look at other

An early rendering of Disneyland is sited on a plot of land across the street from the Disney Studios. Luckily, the concept of the Park outgrew the available space just before the state of California decided to build a freeway through this very spot.

locations as the project took on its own momentum. They looked at Descanso Gardens, California's famous botanical display. One of Walt's early candidates was the police pistol range in the city of Chatsworth, just north of the Studio. The area, while within striking distance of the rapidly developing townships of Southern California, was quiet and idyllic, offering a small brook, rolling hills, and plenty of trees. Then the staff found a place further north, up by Calabasas, in a big, beautiful valley. It has been said that Roy Disney bought some forty acres on margin right in front of the land under consideration in order to protect it.

It finally became clear that such hit or miss methods were doomed to fail,

In the WED design shop, scale model brontosauruses watch over the development of their Primeval World in 1966.

and in July 1953 the Stanford Research Institute was called in. Its point man, or lead scout, Harrison "Buzz" Price, immediately called for a more scientific approach to the problem. He and his team examined every variable for the most suitable property in Southern California. They studied the local climate differences and found the coastal regions clearly cooler in the summer and warmer in the winter than the smog-plagued inland valleys of Los Angeles. Palos Verdes looked inviting but the high costs of coastal real estate ruled it out and, besides, Disney did not want the implication of the tawdry waterfront amusement pier to touch his project. The search for a suitable site continued.

"IMAGINEERING" THE DREAM

At the same time that the property search was under way, an entirely different kind of search was taking place—a talent search for people who could deal with the "real world" aspects of the Disneyland project, its engineering and construction. Harper Goff was temporarily lost to another project, art directing what would be one of Disney's greatest films, *20,000 Leagues Under the Sea*. Unfortunately, this was a case of robbing Peter to pay Paul. If the dream was ever to be realized, a staff had to be built that would be fully dedicated to designing the Park.

Walt retained the architectural firm of Pereira and Luckman to work on concepts and master-planning. Then he hired art director Richard Irvine away from 20th Century-Fox to act as liaison between the Disney people and the architects. Irvine had worked with Disney during the war on *Victory Through Air Power*, and he had a keen sense of what Walt had in mind. He had heard him speak about his idea for a Disney Studio tour many years earlier.

After a few preliminary meetings, Irvine concluded that the people who could best design Disneyland were on Disney's own staff. He felt instinctively that motion-picture art directors, with their know-how and theatrical experience, probably had the best qualifications to put Disney's ideas into concrete form. (Welton Becket, a longtime Disney friend and a famed architect in his own right, had already given Walt a similar opinion.) Irvine strongly recommended that Walt hire and train his own staff.

Walt Disney Productions, by now a public company, did not give its undivided support to Walt's idea for a new amusement park. To quiet the grumblers—and to carry out his plans unimpeded—Disney formed a new corporation, Walt Disney Inc., in 1953, and paid its expenses out of his own pocket as an act of faith in his Disneyland concept. Later, Walt Disney Inc. was changed to WED Enterprises, an acronym for Walter Elias Disney, to avoid possible objections by shareholders of Walt Disney Productions to the use of the Disney name. It became the designing and engineering arm for Disneyland, and later for other themed attractions.

Walt recruited from within the regular Disney organization as well as from the outside. From within his own Studio, Disney hand-picked people who were accustomed to communicating visually and who were instilled with a spirit of innovation. Ken Anderson rejoined the project upon completion of his work on *Sleeping Beauty*. Harper Goff returned with John Hench after they had wrapped up *20,000 Leagues*. Outstanding Disney artists Claude Coats, Herb Ryman, and Marc Davis also contributed significantly to the Disneyland design at one time or another.

Richard Irvine brought his close associates at Fox, art directors Marvin Davis and Bill Martin, on board. Davis, like Ken Anderson, had a degree in architecture.

The WED staff became a harmonic blend of talents that was unparalleled in the entertainment industry. It consisted of designers, architects, writers,

This concept sketch for Plaza Gardens (above) was executed in 1956.

From the beginning, Main Street has remained a street for strollers, where "the pedestrian is king" (left; opposite, below, left and right). It often hosts special traffic, such as the parade (opposite, above) that unleashed one of the largest balloon releases in history to salute the thirtieth anniversary of Disneyland in 1985.

artists, sculptors, engineers, creators of special effects, and imaginative people from many other disciplines. The key prerequisites: open eyes and open minds for radically new ideas. The WED people would not be working in the two-dimensional world of film. They would "Imagineer" in the three-dimensional world of Disneyland.

Irvine remembered, "We just started dreaming a lot of storyboards with notes on them, the way they do in typical Disney fashion." Walt said, "Heavens! The dream's wide open. There's nothing cut or dried about it."

THE LANGUAGE OF VISION

John Hench, a key Disney designer for nearly a half-century, was a close associate of Walt throughout most his career. He even resembled Walt closely enough to cause more than one case of mistaken identity when they were together in public (a situation embarrassing for Hench and irritating for Disney). Hench found that Disney always had a knack for putting "little touches of humanity" in everything he did, from *Snow White* to *Fantasia* to nature films. Walt's new task was to apply his feelings for people with the same skill in his new art form called Disneyland.

Hench calls it "the language of vision" that gave Disney's characters such great popularity. He points out that Mickey Mouse's appeal has at least as much to do with his body shape as his personality. All circles, all round, all harmless, all nonthreatening, unlike Mickey's early, and less successful rival, Felix the Cat, whose sharp, angular lines communicated a subliminal message of threat or danger.

The language of vision in Disneyland was far more complex, but it had the same psychological underpinnings. Visual elements would all be designed to complement one another (nonthreatening) rather than compete (threatening) as they often do in the outside world. "Most urban environments," Hench says, "are basically chaotic places, as architectural and graphics information scream at the citizen for attention. This competition results in disharmonies and contradictions that serve to cancel each other. A journey down almost any urban street will quickly place the visitor into visual overload as all of the competing messages merge into a kind of information gridlock."

In marked contrast, Hench refers to Walt's concept for Disneyland as an extension of Walt's sense of theater. That is to say, the visual elements are laid out as an orderly progression of ideas similar to scenes in a motion picture. "A film makes sense to the audience because the director takes them from scene one to scene two and so on, in a logical flow of events and relationships. If the director were to leapfrog from scene one to scene fifty-two, it would be like sending the audience out for dinner in the middle of the film." At Disneyland, Walt's sense of order would prevail.

THE AMUSEMENT PARK SURVEY

As the Disney designers began to solidify concepts, they needed to survey what had already been done in other parklike entertainment projects. Walt had traveled extensively in Europe in earlier years and had grown quite fond of Copenhagen's Tivoli Gardens. He had also been impressed by Greenfield Village, in Dearborn, Michigan. He dispatched Harper Goff and his wife to Dearborn to gather data regarding personnel as well as the comments and interests of visitors to the village that commemorates American ingenuity. Others on the WED staff went to the Los Angeles County Fair in Pomona and to Knott's Berry Farm in Buena Park. They spent a great deal of time measuring the walks, checking the traffic flow, seeing how people moved about.

Among the most valuable lessons learned by Disney's staff was what not to do, rather than what to do, as they began to survey amusement parks across the country. They found the parks they visited were, for the most part, casually designed and poorly maintained, and all seemed to feature the same types of rides and surly attendants. The WED designers went to Mount Vernon and to Severton Village, Connecticut. They visited famed Coney Island, and discovered that although it had begun life at the turn of the century in somewhat spectacular fashion, it had lapsed into equally spectacular deterioration. They interviewed park operators as well as equipment manufacturers who, with amazing consistency, recommended the customary Ferris wheel, Lindy Loop, and the predictable midway of barkers, who revel in the hokum of "carny show" hard sell. They also found that nearly all of the amusement parks had expanded in a haphazard manner, which made it impossible to control crowd ingress and egress.

The Disney staff concluded, as a result of their fieldwork, that a single entrance was an unequivocal must, that the elements of their park would need to be laid out in a coherent sequence (much like a motion picture), and that the attractions would all need to be unique to Disney. There would be wide, inviting walkways, plenty of landscaping, and shaded benches to provide relief for tired feet. There would be good food and plenty of entertainment—parades, marching bands, and appearances by the Disney characters. A full-time

Amusement park "experts" advised Walt not to elevate the train station (below) *because guests would refuse to walk up the stairs. He did it anyway.*

Walt gave guests another elevated view from the top deck of the Mark Twain (opposite, above), *overlooking Frontierland. Later on, another elevated transportation system—the Monorail (below)—became a Disney mainstay.*

staff of custodians would patrol the new park to keep the grounds spotless. It would be unlike any other park ever built.

Walt asked several owners of amusement parks to come to the Studio and help define WED's emerging plans for Disneyland. One of them was George Whitney, who operated a park in San Francisco. He was absolutely certain that Disney's idea of an elevated train station at the entrance to the Park was wrong. He believed that people would refuse to climb up the stairs to the train. But Disney was very emphatic about the marquee value of major visual elements, and insisted that they had to be elevated in order to be easily seen. An elevated train ride would be too alluring to pass up.

One constructive point that Disney did pick up quickly from nearly all of the amusement park operators was the need for efficient high-capacity operations. It was very apparent that a few seconds lost in loading each ride vehicle translated into major attendance loss at the end of each day. The plans that followed would ultimately lead to operational standards in a class by themselves for handling large numbers of guests, swiftly, effectively, and courteously.

The Stanford Research Institute staff also visited a variety of attractions, both in the United States and abroad. They studied all the different data that could be considered at that time for the still-loosely defined amusement project. At the National Association of Parks, Pools, and Beaches in Chicago, they cornered seven of the nation's owners of leading amusement parks, and explained Walt's concepts for a clean, friendly family park. The reaction was unanimous. "It can't work." "Undercapacity in its rides." "Too much cost in nonrevenue-producing activities, such as janitorial services." "Income would not support the cost." "It couldn't operate year-round." "It would be the world capital of mechanical breakdown."

All of the conflicting and contradictory data hardly encouraged the Disneyland dream. Nonetheless, the Stanford Research Institute put together a feasibility finding that recommended $11 million of initial investment. That's great, thought Disney, but where would I get that kind of money?

"BROTHER, CAN YOU SPARE A DIME?"

Walt did a lot of things to prod his brother Roy into understanding how serious he was about going forward with the development of Disneyland. He once remarked to a favored confidante, Studio nurse Hazel George, that he wasn't getting anywhere with the Studio financial people about money for

Disneyland. The company was still recovering from losses incurred when World War II closed off its European market. Walt's animated features were becoming more and more expensive to produce, and the Studio had just committed substantial capital to begin the production of live-action features. It was reluctant to invest more money in Walt's amusement park.

Hoping she would cooperate with his unique solution, Walt asked Hazel if she would invest in it. Hazel not only agreed, she also convinced other employees. Together, they formed the Disneyland Boosters and Backers, a highly visible gesture that verified Walt's, and his people's, faith in the Disneyland idea. (He himself had made a similar gesture of commitment earlier in personally financing the entire WED organization.) Walt figured that if Roy saw that the rank-and-file employee had enough faith in Disneyland to authorize payroll deductions, then he too would actively support the project. It turned out that passing the hat was never necessary, but the plan did succeed in further securing Roy's commitment to the project, a commitment that would soon prove vital to the success of Disneyland.

Walt had certainly put himself out on a limb financially. He had sold his home in Palm Springs and had cashed in his personal insurance policy in order to keep the development of Disneyland moving forward in the face of growing skepticism. But such helter-skelter fund-raising ploys would never be sufficient to complete the project. In the final crunch, the financial solution came from another new kid on the entertainment block.

"SMILE, YOU'RE ON TELEVISION"

The early 1950s was a formative period for the infant industry called television. The new entertainment medium consisted chiefly of roller derby, wrestling, old Western movies, and Milton Berle. Most Hollywood studios either dismissed TV as a passing fad or considered it the ultimate enemy. Disney embraced it as the ultimate friend. He saw it as a marvelous device through which he could sell his film products and an essential vehicle for communicating his new Disneyland idea to the nation.

Walt Disney's film success had established his product as a marketable commodity in the new world of television. The two major networks wanted him, but every time they discussed a Disney show, Walt started talking about Disneyland, and they cooled off. Walt was adamant: without an agreement from one of the networks to help finance Disneyland, there would be no television series. NBC's chairman, General David Sarnoff, turned the idea of a Dis-

ney program over to his lieutenants, where it quickly bogged down. Other discussions were held with the talent agency MCA, which tried very hard to put together a television package of Walt Disney and his company under General Foods sponsorship.

Walt also met with Leonard Goldenson and Robert Kintner of fiercely competitive ABC, which was attempting to become the third network.

The first ABC meeting had taken place in June 1951, several years before the announcement of the Disneyland project. Its purpose was to talk to Walt about coming into television. Disney had become a "hot commodity" after producing an extremely successful 1950 Christmas special for NBC. In no time at all, Walt had steered the conversation around to Disneyland and described his idea. "It was the first I'd heard about it," said Donn Tatum, an ABC executive who later joined the Disney organization and eventually rose to become chairman of the board. "Walt just carried on and on about it, and built a word picture. He didn't have any visual material to refer to. But even so, he drew such a dramatic, vivid word description that I left with a great deal of enthusiasm. But our people seemed not to understand what he was talking about."

Two years later, in September 1953, the Park's design effort was gaining

The very first rendering of Disneyland (opposite) as we know it today. Artist Herb Ryman made this sketch over a weekend under Walt's direction. Roy Disney then took it to New York, where it played an instrumental role in securing the financing necessary to build the Park.

momentum, and Disney decided it was time to turn again to television for financial backing for Disneyland. This time, Walt called on Roy to make the presentation. Recalling his earlier inability to communicate the concept to the networks, Walt decided that Roy would need to be armed with visual materials. Walt wanted a big, impressive rendering that showed an aerial view of the projected park.

Herb Ryman was a remarkable artist who had worked with Walt in the 1940s and then had gone to 20th Century-Fox to work as an illustrator-sketch artist. He also had been working summers with the Ringling Brothers Circus. One Saturday morning in September 1953, he got a phone call from Dick Irvine. "We're over here at the Disney Studio," he said, "and Walt wants to talk to you." Ryman was very curious. Walt grabbed the phone and told him to get to the Studio as fast as he could. When he arrived, Disney briefed him on the Disneyland concept. "My brother Roy is going to New York Monday morning. He's got to get the idea of this place across to the financiers." Walt described the large rendering of Disneyland that was needed to illustrate Roy's sales pitch.

Impossible, thought Ryman, there just wasn't enough time. But Walt was unrelenting. "I'll stick right with you through the whole time," he promised.

"Where have you got the designs?" asked Ryman.

"You're going to do them," Walt responded.

"Oh, no I'm not," Ryman snapped. "I'm not going to be called in on Saturday morning to do something this complex by Monday. It'll embarrass both you and me. I'm not going to make a fool of myself."

Disney was at once persuasive and pitiful, remembered Ryman. "Like a little boy who wants something. But I didn't have anything to lose. I knew I couldn't do a good job, but if he wanted to stay up all Saturday night and all Sunday night, I figured I could do it, too."

Ryman's mother always kept a diary of his assignments. On Sunday, September 24, 1953, she wrote, "Herbert is helping Walt to do a map of an amusement park. Roy Disney is going to New York soon to talk to the money people about helping to finance Disneyland."

There has probably never been a more intense period in Disneyland design history than the weekend that Disney and Ryman spent together. Walt was fully prepared to art direct the large, conceptual illustration, combining ideas that had already been developed with flashes of inspiration that came to him on this "lost weekend."

"This is a magic place," Walt said. "The important thing is the castle. Make it tall enough to be seen from all around the Park. It's got to keep people oriented. And I want a hub at the end of Main Street, where all the other lands will radiate from, like the spokes in a wheel. I've been studying the way people go to museums and other entertainment places. Everybody's got tired feet. I don't want that to happen in this place. I want a place for people to sit down and where old folks can say, 'You kids run on. I'll meet you there in a half hour.' Disneyland is going to be a place where you can't get lost or tired unless you want to."

Herb drew as Walt talked. He laid out a roughly oval shape, and put Walt's castle near the center. There would be just one entrance to the Park, with an elevated train station rising above. The entrance would lead to Main Street U.S.A., a re-creation of a typical turn-of-the-century American town, and Main Street would lead to the central "hub" of Disneyland, where visitors could choose to enter one of the Park's four realms.

Ahead loomed the castle, and across its drawbridge sat Fantasyland, home of Snow White, Peter Pan, and all the Disney characters. Moving left around the hub, Herb drew a log stockade to mark the entrance of Frontierland, home of Davy Crockett and the American Wild West. Further down, he drew a jungle canopy that covered the entrance to Adventureland, home of True-Life Adventures into the mysterious, uncharted civilizations of the world. And finally, on the opposite side of the hub, Herb drew the futuristic World of Tomorrow, soon to be known as Tomorrowland.

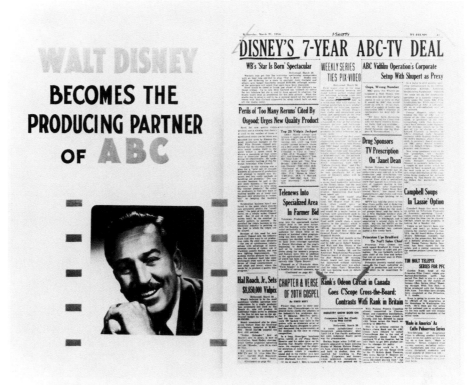

A few days later, with the completed sketch in hand, Dick Irvine landed in New York with Roy Disney. Together, they had a luncheon meeting with ABC's Leonard Goldenson. After studying the Disneyland concept as it was clearly and realistically pictured in the Ryman rendering, he said, "Well, tell Walt that he can have what he wants. We're all ready to go with him." In return for a $500,000 investment and a series of guaranteed loans, ABC would receive a one-third ownership of Disneyland park—and a weekly television series from Walt.

The importance of that New York meeting can't be overstated. With the debut of his weekly ABC series in 1954, Disney was now in television in a big and consistent way. He would host each show himself, introducing live and animated features from each of the four lands that would make up Disneyland. There would be cartoons from Fantasyland, and True-Life Adventure films from Adventureland. Frontierland's Davy Crockett would soon become a national phenomenon, and noted rocket pioneer Wernher Von Braun would launch viewers into outer space from Tomorrowland.

Television was exactly the medium Walt needed to tell the world about his new Park. Every few weeks, Walt planned to present "progress updates" on Project Disneyland, which would show the Park under construction and give the viewers sneak peeks at the attractions-to-be. Now that Walt had financial momentum on his side, and the attention of a nationwide television audience, he had convincing evidence for the banking community that his long-elusive dream could indeed be turned into a money-making proposition.

CHAPTER TWO

"Heigh-Ho, Heigh-Ho, It's Off to Work We Go"

In the lexicon of youth, there is no such word as "fail." Certainly we have all had this confidence at one time in our lives, though most of us lose it as we grow older. Perhaps, because of my work, I've been lucky enough to retain a shred of this youthful quality. But sometimes, as I look back on how tough things were, I wonder if I'd go through it again. I hope I would.

When I was twenty-one, I went broke for the first time. I slept on chair cushions in my "studio" in Kansas City and ate cold beans out of a can. But I took another look at my dream and set out for Hollywood. Foolish? Not to a youngster. An older person might have had too much "common sense" to do it. Sometimes I wonder if "common sense" isn't another way of saying "fear." And fear too often spells failure.

WALT DISNEY

Preceding pages: *Scaffolding encases Sleeping Beauty Castle during its construction in 1955. The stones at the top of the castle were carved in diminishing scale, creating a forced perspective that makes the castle appear taller than it really is.*

Walt Disney's Imagineers translated design sketches, such as this one of Main Street (bottom), *into three-dimensional models* (below) *in order to plan carefully the Park's overall layout.*

Never before had Walt Disney taken on a project with such potential for both fear and failure. Walt had committed to begin his weekly television series in the fall of 1954 and to open Disneyland the following summer—less than two years away. Certainly, thanks to his brilliant track record in animated and live-action films, he had reason enough for confidence. But this project was different: his audience was to be taken out of its theater seats and invited to "step into the screen." Walt would be taking the greatest Disney motion-picture stories and translating them into three-dimensional reality.

Disneyland was to be the first amusement park with a theme: an environmental entertainment experience in which architecture, landscaping, characters, food, merchandise, and even the costumes the employees wear and the roles they play would all blend together in a harmonious motif. And that harmony would create a world of fantasy that could be found nowhere else. "I don't want the public to see the world they live in while they're in the Park," Disney told his designers. "I want them to feel they are in another world."

A NEW WIENIE AND A NEW PERSPECTIVE

It was finally time for the Disney designers to move beyond the conceptual development of Walt's "family park" and commit to the actual, detailed design of a working Disneyland.

The WED staff had profited greatly from its earlier surveys of amusement parks around the country. After studying the "Pike" at Long Beach, they noticed that the main thoroughfares always attracted a throng of pedestrians, while anything off the main drag suffered a great decline in traffic. This observation led to what Disney designers have referred to as the "miracle of the hub." Having already decided that Disneyland would have just one entrance, the WED staff created Main Street as a long entrance corridor that could absorb large numbers of visitors during the peak hours. They also realized that they would need a large visual magnet (called a marquee in design parlance) at the far end of the street, to function as a sort of beckoning finger that would draw people toward it. Walt's favorite term for this attracting device was "wienie," meaning a reward held out in front of people to keep them moving toward their goal. "Sleeping Beauty Castle" at the entrance to Fantasyland would be served up as the first wienie.

Disneyland from the air in the late 1970s (opposite, below) *still bore a striking resemblance to the earliest master plans drawn a quarter of a century earlier* (opposite, above). *The central hub was planned to connect the major lands of Disneyland, making it easy to find one's way around without getting lost or confused. From the very beginning, Disney insisted that the visual centerpiece of his Park would be Sleeping Beauty Castle* (right).

As the guests moved down the street, attracted to the castle, they would arrive at a large hub, from which roads to the other lands radiated like the spokes of a wheel. Again a wienie was carefully chosen to act as a visual magnet at the far end of each road. A towering rocketship was selected for Tomorrowland, a stern-wheel riverboat for Frontierland, a foreboding portal graced with spears and human skulls for Adventureland. "The Hub," said Disney, "gives people a sense of orientation. They know where they are at all times. And it saves a lot of walking."

Another remarkable feature of Disneyland could have been accomplished only by the experienced motion-picture art directors whom Walt hired to replace those first architects. Film designers, long accustomed to dealing with the confined spaces of studio sound stages, were masters at using tricks of scale to make buildings appear much taller or more distant. Through forced perspective, they could create subtly diminishing changes in scale, especially vertical scale, so that a building narrowing toward its top seemed to tower much higher than its true height. It was the only way their sets could accommodate buildings two or three stories tall within a limited space and still leave enough clearance for the sound stage's lighting grids above.

For Disneyland, this talent for forcing perspective and changing scale was employed everywhere. It worked in scaling down the steam train, riverboat, castle, Main Street buildings, and many other elements that in full scale would have overpowered and thus destroyed the believability of Disneyland. Walt wanted his Park to be intimate and friendly and, at the same time, to be a special world where one could suspend disbelief.

Walt signals his pleasure at the controls of the full-size Lilly Belle, one of the Disneyland trains.

One of the most important elements in the Park was, of course, Walt's steam train. Roger Broggie had a head start on the design of the locomotive since he already had the plans from Walt's miniature backyard engine, the Lilly Belle. Broggie determined that in keeping with the intimate scale of Disneyland, the train track should be standard narrow gauge. That meant a three-foot-wide track, and by the time he scaled up the Lilly Belle to that width, the one-eighth-scale train was five times larger. This gave birth to one of the earliest Disneyland myths: for some reason, since the train was now five-eighths scale, it came to be known that all of Disneyland was built in the same scale. Absolutely not true. With the exception of the Main Street horseless carriages and the *Mark Twain* riverboat, the rest of Disneyland was executed not in five-eighths scale but in whatever scale the art directors deemed appropriate to the intimate ambience of the Park. Main Street, for example, was built to a scale that "looked good reduced in proportion," said Dick Irvine. "The first floor of its buildings is about 90 percent full-size. The second floor is around 80 percent, and so forth, so that your eye is deceived with the feeling of looking up at exaggerated vertical space as well as looking at Main Street horizontally."

Meanwhile, the search for a place to build all these ideas took on new urgency.

The E. P. Ripley (foreground) and the C. K. Holliday (background, in shed) arrive at Disneyland, ready for their trial run on July 4, 1955.

Looking for a site for the new park, Disney personnel scoured all of Southern California before settling on orange-grove country in Anaheim, which all studies located in the path of a freeway-inspired growth boom. These aerial photographs show Disneyland in early 1954, prior to the start of construction (above); slowly rising from the sandy orange groves in 1955 (center); and beginning to take shape, as a twenty-foot-high earthen berm prepares to seal out the outside world (below).

THE ORANGE TREE CONNECTION

Teenager Ron Dominguez didn't have any idea what the men were doing in the area. He had noticed strange cars passing by slowly while the occupants studied his mother's orange groves. She had been born on the property in 1898. When she was a teenager, she lost her father just after he had replanted the land from walnut trees to orange groves. For more than four decades, the Dominguez family had tended their orange groves.

Nobody knew whom the inquisitive strangers were representing at the time, but the family did find out that they were looking to purchase the old Dominguez property, along with the adjacent groves of sixteen other landowners. Quietly, agreements were made, even as press releases trumpeted the news that Disney had chosen land in the San Fernando Valley, fifty miles north of the Dominguez ranch, for his "special project." The seemingly endless search for a suitable site for Disneyland had been concluded, all right, but *this* was the real land acquisition. This was Anaheim, California, home of the famed Jack Benny jokes of radio, home of so many orange groves that the entire area was appropriately named Orange County.

"Buzz" Price and the Stanford people had concluded that Southern California was going to expand southeastward, toward Orange County. Their number-one site selection for the Disney park was near the intersection of Harbor Boulevard and the emerging Santa Ana Freeway—right in the middle of Ron Dominguez's family grove. For Ron Dominguez, it would mean something very special one day. His family home would remain as a Disneyland administration building for many years, and Ron himself would later join the Disneyland venture and eventually become vice-president of park operations.

AN INAUSPICIOUS START

Walt was there along with his hand-picked staff when ground was broken in July 1954. The plans were carefully laid. The landscape designers had thoroughly and meticulously inspected every tree in the Disney orange groves, with the purpose of saving as many as possible for the overall design of the Park.

A foolproof method had been devised to sort out the trees in the grove. Tie a green ribbon around the old orange tree, and it would be spared the bulldozer's blade, but a red ribbon would mean "this tree is cleared for clearance." On ground-breaking day, the bulldozer roared across the landscape, leveling red- and green-ribboned trees indiscriminately. Who could have foreseen that the bulldozer operator would be colorblind?

It was an inauspicious beginning for the dream called Disneyland. But it posed only a minor problem to retired Admiral Joseph Fowler, who had been recruited by Walt to head up the Park's construction. A man accustomed to confronting major challenges, Fowler had built ships in China just before World War II and had run the massive, overwhelmingly busy San Francisco Navy Yard during the war. He was known by those close to him as "Admiral Can-Do," and the Disneyland construction site called for every bit of his experience and expertise for the next full year.

One of Fowler's earliest challenges involved making Walt understand the requirements for new construction. Disney was on top of everything and everyone. He quickly learned to read construction plans, and was soon reading them better than anyone on the site. He knew where every pipe was located, the height of each building, and all the other details of the Park's construction. But he found it very difficult to understand the necessity for certain costly building materials and methods. As a longtime filmmaker, Walt had imagined that Disneyland would be built more like a motion-picture set, on a temporary basis. He had to be introduced to the real world of occupancy regulations and building codes.

One day, on a walk-through of the construction site with Fowler and Dick Irvine, Disney became furious when he saw the amount of concrete that was being poured for the Main Street train station foundation. "By the time Joe gets through burying all our money underground," he snapped, "we won't have a thing left for the show!" They then headed for the Adventureland site, only to be faced with still another massive concrete job, as steel bars began to form what appeared to be a large rock outcropping along the jungle river. (This later became one of the most popular features of the Jungle Cruise, the journey under Schweitzer Falls.) An incensed Disney was convinced that Fowler was using his park as the cement contractor's full-employment act of 1955. And if this didn't exasperate Walt enough, a nearby construction worker was ready to provide the *coup de grâce*.

"Tiny" was a water-car operator who weighed more than three hundred pounds and had as large an appetite for pranks as he did for food. He took a devilish delight in catching some unwary victim in the jungle territory with his high-powered water hose. As fate would have it, Walt came around the corner, already steaming, only to be cooled down by the drenching full force of Tiny's water stream. Tiny's paycheck was soon smaller than his name.

ADVENTURELAND: "IT'S A REAL JUNGLE OUT THERE"

While Fowler dealt with Walt's consternation at the real world of building, Harper Goff found himself doing a lot of hand-holding with the construction workers, especially in Adventureland, as they adjusted to building a world of fantasy. Most of them had built conventional, standard projects: office buildings, hospitals, schools, warehouses. Faced with blueprints calling for African ruins, native huts, and ancient shrines all along the edge of a huge, winding ditch that was supposed to be a riverbed, they needed constant direction and reassurance. Goff's own confidence wasn't bolstered, either, when he kept losing his surveying stakes to the Jeeps, trucks, and bulldozers as they crawled over the landscape that was trying to become a jungle.

"The spirit of adventure is often linked with exotic tropic places," Walt once said, describing those early days of design. "To create a land which would make this dream reality, we pictured ourselves far from civilization, in the remote jungles of Asia and Africa. The result is Adventureland, 'the wonderland of nature's own design.'"

The major attraction in Adventureland—in fact, the only attraction in Adventureland on opening day—would be a cruise down the jungle rivers of the world. Guests would board their launches from a dock located in the heart of a small trader's village, hewn out of the jungle landscape. The shops in the village would offer something for everyone: a variety of tropical supplies, jungle hats, rubber snakes, and shrunken heads. There would even be a small shooting gallery where armchair hunters could test their aim before setting out into the uncharted wild.

The adventures in Adventureland, however, hadn't always been set in the jungle. It was Harper Goff's infatuation with the motion picture *The African Queen*, starring Katharine Hepburn and Humphrey Bogart, that inspired the concept of a cruise down tropical rivers of the world. Harper knew his jungle river cruise would be far more exciting to the public than a cruise down exclusively American rivers like the Suwannee, one of the original ideas for Adventureland. But zoologists had convinced him and Walt that their initial idea of using live animals was impractical: most of the animals would be asleep during the Park's operating hours. Undiscouraged, Walt simply approached the problem from the other side. His special-effects group at the Studio had animated a remarkably realistic "giant squid" for the film *20,000 Leagues Under the Sea*. It shouldn't be much more difficult to create lifelike elephants, crocodiles, and monkeys, which would be wide-awake when needed. Further-

An early concept of Adventureland featured the Jungle Cruise (opposite, above, left). Landscape designer Bill Evans translated such early Jungle Cruise sketches into a "Hollywood jungle" that became the home of towering giraffes (opposite, below) and, eventually, of sophisticated animated African bull elephants (above). In the late 1970s, the Jungle River Cruise was celebrated with a silk-screened poster comprised of more than fifty colors (opposite, above, right).

more, Goff had pointed out that the animals filmed in or near the river in *The African Queen* were never totally clear of the water or the underbrush. If Walt staged his animals the same way, he could hide the tracks and mechanical controls required for the animation.

Laboring on the Studio special-effects stage, mechanical wizard Bob Mattey began creating crocodiles that could swim and submerge realistically. Unfortunately, the murky Jungle Cruise river soon gave the mechanical marvels a death blow, encasing each croc in a claylike ceramic coating while causing their bronze mechanical innards to grind themselves to pieces with a fine, abrasive silicate that was suspended in the water. For the most part, though, it seemed that the more complicated animation machinery continued to function quite well. Simple and normally reliable electric motors, however, gave Mattey almost endless trouble.

While most of the animals were built and tested at the Studio, some of the larger ones were made right at the Park. One 900-pound mechanical elephant would be delivered the night before the Park opened, to be installed in the river in pitch darkness after a night watchman unwittingly turned off the work lights.

Perhaps the greatest challenge in Adventureland was creating a home for Bob Mattey's cast of mechanical critters, a believable, living, breathing humid "jungle" that could survive and thrive in the arid, desert-like climate of Southern California. Bill Evans, the chief landscape architect, had traveled a great deal in the tropical regions of the world, where he found few actual jungles. When he did encounter the classic jungle, such as along the Amazon River, he found it to be as endlessly monotonous on the one hand as it was spectacular on the other.

At Disneyland, Evans decided to create a Hollywood jungle, the type the armchair traveler who has never been to the tropics visualizes—man-eating plants, bananas, sixty-foot-high bamboos, and giant palms. Ironically, perhaps the greatest source of plant material for Evans's "far-off exotic jungle" turned out to be the nearest and most unlikely of locations, the pathways of Southern California's rapidly growing freeways. His extensive landscaping experience throughout the area (including the Disney estate at Holmby Hills) had given Evans a vast storehouse of knowledge about the location of mature trees and other major plant material. Armed with plans for the expanding freeway system, Evans's crews snatched palm after giant palm from the jaws of advancing bulldozers. With these, they began to create an instant jungle canopy that otherwise would have taken years to grow.

Probably no one in the history of landscape design ever faced the challenge that Evans and his team encountered. They had to create not only a jungle for Adventureland in the Southern California desert but also richly multitextured pine forests for Frontierland, formal floral gardens for Main Street's celebration of the 1890s, and dozens of other "miniscapes" to complement the many Disneyland environments. In addition, because the Park had to operate year-round in order to be successful, they had to make all these landscapes "evergreen." The starkness of fall and winter in many parts of the world, marked by legions of bare tree trunks and branches, would not be acceptable here.

"For us," Evans says, "trees are what clay is for the sculptor or the paint palette to the artist." But he understood that his mission was to support the Disneyland architecture, not compete with it. Evans actually considered himself an extension of the art director's vision. "We wanted to do everything we could to enhance the illusion, whatever it might be," he said. "But we always knew that our work was not the main event. We tried to create designs of growing things to look as if you had sort of stumbled across them and found them there naturally. Any time our landscaping designs call attention to themselves, I feel that we've failed in our mission."

Evans was also asked to produce landscaped environments with shade trees, where guests could relax on benches and enjoy relief from the summer sun. In addition, the landscaping provides the kinetics that create a counterpoint to the Park's architecture. "Unlike the buildings," he says, "the landscaping is alive. The trees respond to the breeze, they have life and motion, and they're usually filled with twittering birds and rustling leaves."

Shutting out the twentieth century was still another of Evans's assignments. A twenty-foot earthen berm had been formed around the Park, shielding it from the outside world. Evans's job was to reinforce the isolation with thousands of plants. No wonder Hollywood columnist Hedda Hopper wrote, "Walt Disney has depleted our nurseries from Santa Barbara to San Diego." And no wonder that Disneyland would later become classified in landscaping circles as a botanical garden.

FRONTIERLAND: THE CASE OF THE DISAPPEARING RIVER

"All of us have cause to be proud of our country's history," Walt said in describing his plans for Frontierland. "Here you can return to frontier America, from the Revolutionary War era to the final taming of the great southwest."

The Mark Twain *hull was fabricated at the Todd Shipyards in Long Beach, California* (left), *and the upper decks of the* Mark Twain, *assembled in dry dock in Frontierland in 1955, were fitted to the hull in Disneyland* (opposite).

In its early days, Frontierland would offer rides aboard stagecoaches, Conestoga wagons, and pack mules, exploring the dusty trails through the backwoods of the land. Frontier pioneers could find refreshment at the nearby Golden Horseshoe Saloon, home of the wildest show in the West, and pick up supplies and souvenirs in the shops of the old Western town.

But the biggest attraction in the land would be a scenic journey down the Rivers of America aboard the *Mark Twain* stern-wheeler. As usual, the development of the *Mark Twain* and the river would not be without problems.

One of Walt's walk-throughs of the Frontierland construction site brought another heavy case of "Walt woes." Still horrified by the great cement extravagance of Main Street and the jungle, he was startled by a massive excavation along what was to be the Rivers of America. Joe Fowler viewed the hole, a dry dock-to-be for the *Mark Twain* during its important maintenance overhauls, as an operational necessity. To Walt Disney, it looked more like the excavation for King Tut's tomb. "By the time you get through with that damn ditch, we won't have any land left!" exclaimed Disney. For a long time thereafter, he called it "Joe's Ditch" and gave him, perhaps, one final sarcastic jab by officially dubbing it "Fowler's Harbor." Secretly, though, he must have applauded the objective of the dry dock. The *Mark Twain* riverboat was possibly his favorite project. He felt so strongly about it that when corporate funding fell short for building the stately stern-wheeler, Disney paid for the construction out of his own pocket.

Walt's "Queen of the River" was the first paddle-wheeler built in the United States in fifty years. It actually utilized two "shipyards"—a local shipbuilding facility constructed the 105-foot hull while the Disney Studio fabricated the upper deck units. Miracle of miracles, the parts fit together perfectly at Disneyland to form a five-eighths-scale, 159-ton replica of the great steamboats that once plied the mighty, muddy Mississippi between St. Louis and New Orleans.

The original Disneyland brochure sketch for Frontierland (above) gave a wonderful idea of the place, but the reality was even better (left).

The "Golden Horseshoe Revue" in Frontierland (below), which opened in 1955, was the wildest show in the West. By the time the original Revue closed in October 1986, it had been entered into the Guinness Book of World Records as the longest-running stage production in history, having given more than fifty thousand performances.

At one point, Fowler's pet dry dock almost became permanently dry, along with the rest of the Rivers of America. The occasion was "fill-the-river day." A construction supervisor remembers his glow of pride as the massive pressure valves opened to admit a torrent of water rushing into the Frontierland riverbed . . . then his feeling of desperation as the river promptly leaked its contents into the sandy soil. The gooey soil stabilizer they had added to avoid just this problem had worked well on earthen dams before, but the idea just didn't hold water in this former orange grove. Quickly, Fowler located a major source of clay, and truckload after truckload was brought in with which to line the riverbed. By the next fill-the-river day, it was leak-proof.

To many people, the frontier meant cowboys, covered wagons, and horses. Walt himself loved horseback riding, and in his younger days had found the best outlet for it in polo playing, a sport vigorously pursued by many of Hollywood's top film personalities. For many years the Burbank area surrounding the Disney Studio had been horse country, with riding trails and stables scattered throughout the community. So it was only natural that Walt took an instant liking to Owen Pope, horse-exhibitor extraordinary.

Harper Goff had first seen Pope's horse show at the Pan Pacific Auditorium in Los Angeles back in 1951 and convinced Walt to do likewise. It wasn't long before Walt invited Owen and his wife Dolly to the Studio and, in his inimitable way, gave them the grand picture for his Disneyland dream. He talked about the critical need to begin to develop a herd of Disney horses and ponies to be used in Frontierland and Main Street. The Popes soon became residents on the Studio lot, where Owen began the task of building a mini-ranch of horse stalls, wagons, and coaches. When the Park's construction began, the Popes moved permanently to the site and created a pony farm. By opening day, a wonderful and widely diverse herd of two hundred horses, ponies, and mules were ready and—mostly—willing and able to go to work. (The mules did everything they could to live up to their well-known reputation for orneriness.)

FANTASYLAND: THE *OTHER* HERD

Bruce Bushman also cultivated horses for Disneyland. His herd, born in Germany, numbered fifty-five and ranged from sixty to eighty years in age. The Bushman horses were of the classic, hand-carved, wooden carrousel species and had been corralled under the pier at Coney Island and brought west to Disneyland. After a six-decades' accumulation of paint was removed, they were carefully restored and installed on Fantasyland's King Arthur Carrousel.

Bushman, whom Disney assigned to develop many of the other rides for Fantasyland, was a big, husky man. Walt took one look at him and decided that his proportions would guide the pattern for all the seats at the Park. "If it fits you, Bruce, it'll fit anybody," said Walt, eyeing the broad Bushman beam. So all seats throughout the park were built to be more than ample for one parent and a child.

For Bushman, Fantasyland seemed to be a world of constant change. He saw the Casey Jr. Circus Train chug up its first test hill and tip backward, prompting a grade change from 45 percent to 25 percent. Mr. Toad's Wild Ride was toned down to be a little less wild. It had been a roller-coaster ride at its inception, but it was made less threatening because Walt was concerned that grown-up family members would probably shy away from a too-thrilling "white-knuckle" toad ride.

Two of Bushman's ideas competed with each other for a spot on the Disneyland list of attractions. One was a "Monstro the Whale" ride, adapted from the episode in *Pinocchio* in which the marionette is swallowed by a whale. A small craft was to be taken into Monstro's mouth, lifted to the whale's throat, and hurled down a watery path to a pond below. The other idea was a crocodile aquarium, where guests would walk through the animal's mouth and stroll in a simulated underwater environment to view collections of exotic fish. Walt pondered which would be more fun, being eaten by Pinocchio's whale or Peter Pan's crocodile. Monstro the Whale won, and, to this day, he consumes canal boats at the entrance to Storybook Land.

Walt later described a visit to Fantasyland. "What youngster hasn't dreamed of flying with Peter Pan over moonlit London?" he asked. "Here in the 'happiest kingdom of them all,' you can journey with Snow White through the dark forest to the diamond mine of the Seven Dwarfs; flee the clutches of Mr. Smee and Captain Hook with Peter Pan; and race with Mr. Toad in his wild auto ride through the streets of old London Town. The time you spend in this carefree kingdom will be a dream come true—for everyone who is young in heart."

The Fantasyland "dark rides"—"Peter Pan's Flight," "Snow White's Adventures," and "Mr. Toad's Wild Ride"—gained a touch of magic from Claude Coats's magic touch with color. These attractions were called "dark rides" because they made extensive use of black light, a particular kind of light that makes specially painted scenes glow with an eerie luminescence. Any white clothing worn by the guests also glows strangely in this light.

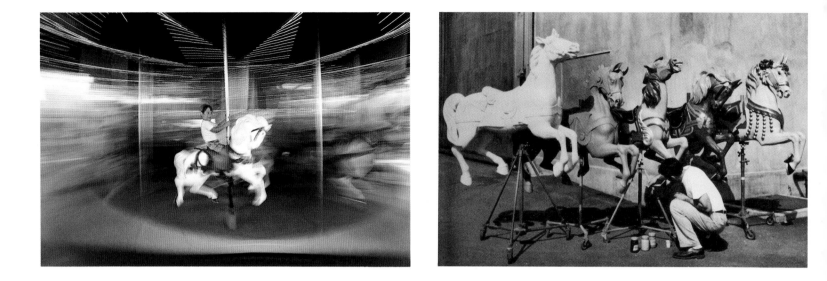

The Fantasyland Carrousel steeds, rescued from disrepair (above, right) *at once-proud Coney Island, were soon prancing at Disneyland* (above, left).

Monstro the Whale consumes another boatload of guests en route to Storybook Land (below).

Casey Jr. Circus Train careens through the miniature Alpine setting of Storybook Land (above). Matterhorn Mountain, not so miniature, rises in the background.

Early Fantasyland sketches, such as the cutaway view of the Peter Pan attraction (below, left) and the early ride concepts (below, right), both of 1954, were constantly refined.

Overleaf: *Construction workers lay the tracks for the Horse-Drawn Streetcars on Main Street in 1955.*

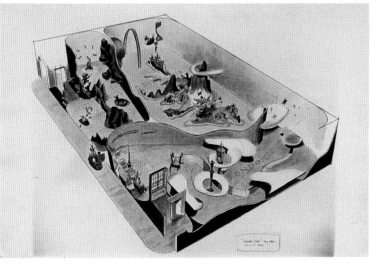

Herb Ryman's castle concept (left) *overcame internal controversy with the help of Walt Disney to be transformed to reality* (below) *through forced-perspective architecture and a healthy dose of art direction in the field.*

Coats had brought stunning moods of color to all of the backgrounds of Disney's animated classic films. Walt employed him to impart the same sense of mood and emotion to the Fantasyland attractions that translated his classic animated films to three-dimensional reality. One by one, the dark rides were given the "Coats touch" of fluorescent colors that lifted them far beyond anything that had ever before been achieved in the scenic medium.

Sleeping Beauty Castle at the entrance to Fantasyland, probably one of the most familiar shapes in the world today, occasioned a great debate as it lay on the drawing board. As in so many other Disneyland designs, forced per-

spective would be used to make the towers seem much taller than they actually were. The castle's stones would gradually be reduced in size, from large ones at the base to small ones at the top of the towers. Inspired by the pinnacled Neuschwanstein castle in Bavaria, several WED designers had created a scaled-down facsimile for Fantasyland.

Herb Ryman, one of the designers, took great exception to copying a famous European landmark. One day, as the designers were arguing the issue, Ryman pointed out that the Bavarian castle faced backward in the Disneyland plan. Moving the pieces of the model around like chess pieces, Ryman picked up the top of the castle, turned it completely around, and set it back down with the turrets facing Main Street. It turned out to be Ryman's lucky day. As the debate raged on, with the model left the way Ryman had placed it, Walt walked into the room and took an instant liking to the idea. End of debate.

Another unusual structure planned for Fantasyland was a giant "Rock Candy Mountain." John Hench, assigned to the project, gathered his henchmen and went to work, creating a large skeletal structure for the table-top scale model of the mountain. They planned on a kind of solidified marshmallow cream for the snow and chocolate for the rock outcroppings. They accumulated a staggering array of real candy bars, gum drops, and other sweets, and applied them to the model's surface. But the more they worked, the more unappealing it began to look.

"It was positively nauseating," said Hench, "and, worst of all, because our building didn't have air conditioning, the whole mountain began to melt. We had to leave the door open and try to ventilate the place to get rid of the odor. It was like a dying candy factory. Then the smell began to attract dozens of birds, flying in and out of the building, pecking away at our mountain." As tenacious as Walt usually was about pursuing ideas, he quietly abandoned his "revolting" Rock Candy Mountain.

TOMORROWLAND: THE LAND THAT TIME (AND BUDGET) ALMOST FORGOT

"Tomorrow can be a wonderful age," Walt Disney once said. "Our scientists today are opening the doors of the Space Age to achievements which will benefit our children and generations to come. In Tomorrowland, you will actually experience what many of America's foremost men of science and industry predict for the world of tomorrow."

It was a foregone conclusion among most of the Disney people, though, that opening day would find Walt's world of tomorrow boarded up. With time and money running out, the best that could be done was to put up some temptingly exciting posters promising things to come for future years. But Walt, determined to get at least some portion of Tomorrowland operating for the nationally televised grand opening, had other ideas.

So, with less than six months to go before the Park opened, work was begun on some of the attractions for his world of tomorrow. Towering above Tomorrowland, the "Rocket to the Moon" would launch guests on a journey into space and back again. Along the promenade leading into Tomorrowland, "Space Station X-1" would invite guests to circle the earth from fifty miles up for a satellite view of America. And "The World Beneath Us" would be explored in a fast-paced animated history of man's quest for energy.

Of all the attractions, Walt felt the "Autopia" was the most important to have ready for the television cameras. It would provide the young and hungry eye of TV with a perfect subject: Hollywood stars and other celebrities roaring past the cameras in miniature Autopia sports cars instead of in the Rolls-Royce and Cadillac convoys that usually signaled gala premieres.

According to Roger Broggie, the Autopia began with the original purpose of giving young children a place where they could learn to drive, the idea being that they would later drive safely on the rapidly growing freeway system. The Autopia roadways were even laid out just like their big brothers in Southern California, with twisting cloverleafs and overpasses.

Broggie's machine shop designed and manufactured thirty-six miniature automobiles, each powered by lawn-mower-type gasoline engines. The Studio then brought in young "test drivers," including Broggie's own children, to try them out. In the first ten days, the thirty-six cars were reduced to six. Instead of learning to drive safely, the kids took "demented delight" in chasing and crashing into one another. After Broggie installed huge springlike bumpers that completely surrounded each car, the fleet's life expectancy skyrocketed—

but the admirable goal of teaching safe driving to California children went by the wayside.

Another Tomorrowland attraction with a Hollywood aura, the "Circarama" theater, outdid anything that Hollywood had to offer by presenting a film on a screen that totally surrounded the audience. A press release of June 27, 1955, described the new process: "An advanced motion-picture development, Circarama, consisting of a continuous image focused on a 360-degree screen, will be introduced at Disneyland Park on July 17th by American Motors Corporation, producer of Hudson, Nash and Rambler automobiles, Kelvinator appliances."

The press release went on in detail about the pioneering new film system, concluding, "'This combination of photographic skills and entertainment talents promises an unusual spectacle for visitors to Disneyland. We're happy to have a part to play in making Circarama possible. As it represents added pleasure and value for the public, sponsorship of the Circarama is another forward step in our program to make American Motors mean more for Americans,' said George Romney, President."

It is not known whether the "car" in Circarama was part of the agreement between Disney and Romney. It is known, however, that a kind of symbiotic relationship developed between Disney and American Motors, Kodak, Richfield, Kaiser Aluminum, TWA, Monsanto, and many other sponsors that would be there for the Park's grand opening. The companies were banking on the association with Disney and their public exposure at the Park and through promotional tie-ins to pay off in both image and sales. The sponsorship association provided Disney with badly needed funds to continue feeding his insatiable appetite for pioneering new forms of entertainment.

Circarama was one of those dreams that needed feeding. After seeing the Cinerama system at the Hollywood Pantages theater, Disney called Broggie and his associate Eustace Lycett, a special-effects and lens expert, to his office. "If they can put three screens together, why can't we do a full circle?" Walt asked.

Eventually, Broggie's team, with the help of Walt's longtime associate, Ub Iwerks, managed to fit eleven 16-millimeter cameras together. Film art director Peter Ellenshaw was dispatched to create a documentary auto tour of the western United States with the Circarama cameras strapped to the top of an American Motors Rambler. But the trip was plagued with problems from the very beginning. On the way to Utah's Monument Valley, the first good bump sent the whole camera system lurching forward. Finding good, smooth

Captain Nemo's magnificent pipe organ, used in Disney's Academy Award–winning film 20,000 Leagues Under the Sea, *became part of an early Tomorrowland exhibit (right). Early Autopia cars were steered by the guests (opposite). Mounting "freeway pileups" led to rail-guided cars by 1965.*

roads in the desert was next to impossible. And finding scenery that was beautiful in a 360-degree sweep was almost as difficult. Time after time Ellenshaw would come upon magnificent mesas and buttes on one side only to discover flat, dull desert and electric power lines on the other.

While shooting the short film, entitled "A Tour of the West," Ellenshaw and his crew drove the car at fifteen to twenty miles per hour. But when they reached stately Wilshire Boulevard in Los Angeles, they wanted to create the illusion of a high-speed chase. They achieved their effect with an old, but effective, Hollywood trick. While they traveled down the street at a sedate twenty miles per hour, they slowed the speed at which the film traveled through the camera. This meant that fewer frames of film were shot, and when these fewer frames were projected back at normal speed, everything looked like it was racing by. "The effect was astonishing," said Ellenshaw. "Suddenly we were hotrodders, racing down Wilshire at a hundred miles per hour, jumping out at green lights, and crashing to a stop only inches from the cars in front."

The Wilshire "race" became the major highlight of a stunningly unique film experience that thrilled audiences from the day Disneyland opened.

Disney had another thriller in mind for Tomorrowland. Ken Anderson had just finished working on the Fantasyland rides when he found himself entered in "the great squid race." Only two weeks before the opening, he got a call from Walt Disney. Walt wanted to get the giant squid from *20,000 Leagues Under the Sea* installed in Tomorrowland's exhibit of the film's set and artwork. "Ken, I've just got to get this squid in there, alive and operating," Disney said. "Swell," thought Anderson. The squid in the film had legions of people, acting as puppet-masters, to operate its cables, wires, and pulleys. He needed to find a different way to get it to wiggle its tentacles.

First he had to have the squid restored. The original skin had been hacked to pieces by the seamen in the film's momentous fight on the deck of the submarine *Nautilus*. It was one of the quickest jobs Bob Mattey ever handled. On Monday, he got the order from Anderson. On Friday, he was installing the giant squid at Disneyland with a whole new set of innards and a new skin.

Mattey then secured a Hudson eight-cylinder engine to create the animation power that had been supplied by the original film crew. Anderson and other artists painted the entire set with fluorescent paint, working impossibly long hours. It was a tight race, but despite their almost superhuman efforts, it soon became apparent to all that the giant squid wouldn't make it across the finish line in time for opening day. (The attraction opened almost three weeks later.)

THE FINAL CONSTRUCTION COUNTDOWN

One morning, Walt was making the two-and-a-half-hour drive from the Studio to the Disneyland site with Herb Ryman. (The freeways were still in a state of becoming in those days.) Ryman, remembering Disney's beautiful Smoke Tree Ranch home, asked Walt if he had spent the weekend in Palm Springs. He soon found out that Walt had sold the home to finance Disneyland. "I need every penny I can get for the Park," Walt replied.

While Joe Fowler did not dip into his own pocket, the financial squeeze haunted him as an incipient disaster from the beginning. "I didn't know a damn thing about what we were getting into. At ground-breaking, I had a budget of four-and-a-half million dollars. That was before we had any plans at all. Two months later, in September, it went up to seven million dollars. In November, it was up to eleven million. We were still talking eleven million dollars in April when I was walking down Main Street with Roy and a representative from Bank of America, who scanned the project and said it looked closer to fifteen million. But by the time opening day had arrived, we had spent seventeen million dollars."

Fowler could not be held responsible for the spiraling costs. The Disneyland site was subjected to a record rainfall in early 1955 that plagued many areas with flooding. And the Park entered the homestretch run for completion with labor strike problems. Orange County's hot-asphalt plants were shut down and picketed. For the last of the Disneyland roads, Fowler had to haul asphalt all the way from San Diego at a staggering, budget-busting cost. Then he faced a plumber's strike that left the Park with a shortage of drinking fountains on opening day, a problem that would later come back to haunt him.

During the final weeks of preparation, old-time amusement park operators once again began to surface, this time not to criticize but to seek employment. Disney and Fowler agreed that they wanted no part of the "carny operators" in the Park. One insulted operator of state fairs in California told Fowler, "Young man, you don't know anything about the amusement business. You're going to fall flat on your face!" Fowler thanked him for calling him "young man," but the answer was still no.

As opening day drew ever closer, most of the key Disney personnel lived near the Park and worked from dawn to late evening. Walt Disney was living *in* the Park, in his apartment overlooking Main Street. Shortly before the Park opened, Walt decided to celebrate his wedding anniversary by throwing an elaborate party in the Golden Horseshoe, the Frontierland re-creation of an Old West dance hall and saloon. The *Mark Twain*, Walt hoped, would be ready to take the party on a voyage around the Rivers of America.

Using the *Mark Twain* that night made Joe Fowler very nervous. He had had a dream the previous night that the river had once again sprung a leak and gone dry. And the stern-wheeler had not yet been tested on the river, leaving a wide opening for Murphy's Law (if anything *can* go wrong, it *will* go wrong). Fowler slipped away from the raucous party an hour before the planned excursion and headed for the ship landing. There he ran into a woman frantically sweeping shavings from the deck. Handing the startled admiral a broom, she said, "Come on, hurry, let's get this thing cleaned up!" Together Fowler and Walt's wife, Lillian, gave the *Mark Twain* a "spit and polish" cleaning for its maiden journey. "Mr. Murphy" did not make the trip. He waited until opening day.

AN OPENING DAY "DISASTER"

The building statistics in the opening day press kit were impressive beyond imagination:

Two million board feet of lumber had been consumed.

Despite strikes, a million square feet of asphalt had paved the streets, some of it still steaming along Main Street.

Five thousand cubic yards of concrete had been poured. And seventy

On opening day, July 17, 1955, these children were the first to cross the drawbridge into Fantasyland.

times that volume in plain old earth had been stacked and compressed into the berm surrounding the Park that kept the outside world truly outside. But none of these things kept "Murphy" and his law outside Disneyland on July 17, 1955.

"It was a madhouse," remembers C. V. Wood. He was a tough-talking Disney construction boss, the former head of the Stanford Research Institute, and the prime recruiter of Admiral Fowler to the Disney team. "We printed either ten or fifteen thousand tickets. But people were counterfeiting the damn things. We even found a guy who had built a ladder and flopped it over the barbed wire fence back where the stables were. You could just walk up and over real easy. He was letting people in for five damn bucks a head."

The party was by invitation only, but all day long people showed up at the main gate uninvited, swearing they were friends of Disney. The guards and ticket-takers were hopelessly confused. One ticket-taker remembers the debacle. "People... people... people! We would open for twenty minutes and then close for twenty minutes."

Nobody knows just how many people got in that day, but more than twice the maximum projected attendance of ten to fifteen thousand is said to have been there, at least half of them party crashers. Dick Irvine took one look at the mob and elected to stay in Fowler's office, safely removed from the fray. One specially invited guest, Walter Knott, chose to brave the throngs. The founder of nearby Knott's Berry Farm, which featured a small "Ghost Town," an early forerunner of Walt's theme-park concept, he wanted to get a look at his competition. If he had mixed feelings about all the attention being given to his new neighbor, they were quickly alleviated when he returned to his place later in the day: instead of finding an empty ghost town, he found that Knott's Berry Farm was also very busy. It would benefit, not wither, through the presence of the new kid on the block. Knott's would eventually become one of the largest amusement parks in the country.

After working all night in the 20,000 Leagues exhibit, Ken Anderson was just sitting down to relax when somebody came rushing up and announced that the power was out on the Mr. Toad attraction. Anderson rushed over to the electrical equipment box and promptly fell asleep. He doesn't remember a thing about the opening.

"The worst thing that happened to us," recalled Wood, "occurred during the live television show. When the program came on, it showed everybody coming underneath the railroad track and into Main Street. But no one realized the asphalt on the street was still hot. The high-heeled shoes that the

women wore literally sank into the pavement. Our 'first ladies' were trapped and had to walk right out of their shoes!"

It was said that never before in television's young history had more than three cameras been used during a show. ABC used twenty-two at Disneyland to capture all the action.

Bob Cummings, Art Linkletter, and Ronald Reagan had formed a telecast triumvirate to host the festivities. "I think that everyone here will one day be as proud to have been at this opening as the people who were there at the dedication of the Eiffel Tower," shouted Cummings into his microphone. The TV cameras performed very well. As planned, they caught star after Hollywood star, including Frank Sinatra and Sammy Davis, Jr., driving on the Autopia. They found comedian Alan Young spinning about on the giant-size teacups in Fantasyland, and discovered actress Irene Dunne futilely trying to break a bottle of water across the bow of the *Mark Twain* in Frontierland.

The telecast seemed to catch every miscue perfectly. At the sound of an ill-timed gunshot, national superhero Davy Crockett (played by Fess Parker on Disney's remarkably popular television show) rode his horse through Bill Evans's newly planted pine forests. A television director gave a wrong cue to a gardener, who turned on the sprinklers just as Parker and his sidekick, Buddy Ebsen, arrived. Still mounted, an exasperated, soaked, and lost Parker later

Walt Disney and California Governor Goodwin Knight lead the opening day parade down Main Street, U.S.A. (below). Later on, Walt formally opened Fantasyland, dedicated "to the young and the young in heart" (opposite).

confronted a Disneyland publicist. "Help me get out of here," he pleaded, "before this horse kills somebody!" Even Walt Disney himself did not escape Murphy's Law on this fateful day. At one point, he was caught live on camera while, thinking he was off, he chatted casually with one of the TV crews.

Reviewing the telecast of the opening day, it appears humorous indeed and refreshingly spontaneous, reflecting the honesty of live video coverage in its early days. Step by step, Walt walked through the opening ceremony of each land, concluding with perhaps the most classically "Disney" land of all, Fantasyland.

It was with the world of fantasy that he had begun his incredible journey nearly three decades earlier, a journey that began with a mouse named Mickey. As the TV cameras looked on, Walt paused near the drawbridge to Sleeping Beauty Castle and read the Fantasyland dedication aloud. "Fantasyland is dedicated to the young and the young in heart, to those who believe when you wish upon a star, your dreams do come true." He then stood up, walked over to the drawbridge, and strolled through Sleeping Beauty Castle, returning to the land he knew best. Although opening day would become notorious among the press—and even among Disney's own employees—as "Black Sunday," Walt knew his dream for Disneyland was no longer just a dream.

CHAPTER THREE

The Infant Years

I could never convince the financiers that Disneyland was feasible, because dreams offer too little collateral.

WALT DISNEY

At birth, Disneyland was a $17 million, twenty-two-attraction infant whose struggles had only just begun. Like all other infants, Walt's brainchild would have to learn to crawl and then to walk before it could run. And like the others, it would stumble often during the process.

BIRTH PAINS

On the day following the problem-ridden "Black Sunday," the general public was admitted to Disneyland for the first time. And just like Black Sunday, this day would not soon be forgotten.

As construction supervisor C. V. Wood hurried from land to land, someone came running up to him and yelled, "We've got a gas leak in Fantasyland!" He checked it out and found, sure enough, gas flames coming right through the asphalt in Fantasyland. Disneyland publicists pleaded with the press not to take pictures of the flames. It worked, but the photographers remained on ladders with cameras cocked for quite a while. (Presumably, they were ready to film the castle if it blew up.) Fowler had the area roped off as Wood desperately grabbed maintenance men armed with shovels to dig up the area in order to find the leak. Fortunately, they found it. Unwilling to take any chances, Wood went from place to place, building to building, gingerly testing each area with lighted matches.

Meanwhile, over at the *Mark Twain* stern-wheeler, the operators learned very quickly about the relationship between crowd behavior and capacity. When they opened the *Mark Twain* to the public, no one had actually established its full capacity. The steam engineer remembers the maiden voyage.

"We just let them keep coming on board until we were close to shipping water over the lower deck. We figured that was enough, so we locked the gates and I started the engines full steam ahead. Things were okay until we got to the back side of Tom Sawyer Island. In those days, there was practically nothing to see. The vegetation was sparse, and there were few scenes along the river bank. And here we had a jillion guests and reporters clamoring all over the boat, trying to find something to look at."

Finally, the boat sailed past a scene worth viewing, a small encampment of Indian tents. "Everyone ran to the starboard side of the boat," the mechanic

continued, "and we started shipping water over the side as we almost tipped over. Then someone pointed out something on the port side and there was a stampede to the other side. The boat rolled and creaked under the strain, as water poured over the deck from the other side. I thought we would never get back to the dock before capsizing." The *Mark Twain* crew quickly set a capacity safety limitation that still stands today.

If things were frantic out in the Park, the situation wasn't much better back at the office. Some Disneyland employees still remember the madcap method of cash collection during those first weeks. In order to get the payroll deposits to the bank on time, main-gate clerks would leave the ticket booths laden with fire buckets filled with all types of money and run to the office. (To the guests, it must have been a bizarre sight indeed.) The clerks dumped each bucket on a large table and the Disney treasurer would count the money. Then, like a relay runner in a race, he would grab the cash and quickly head to the bank to cover the paychecks.

Delivering money in those days was one thing. Getting it counted was another. One cash-control clerk devised an ingenious if not terribly accurate way to count the income. "I was working at a food facility, an automat in

Preceding pages: *Walt oversees the installation of the African Veldt deep in the jungles of Adventureland in 1962.*

Although she has been running flawlessly ever since, the Mark Twain Steamboat *(above) nearly capsized because of overloading on her earliest voyages.*

The old grist mill and rotating water wheel became a landmark of Tom Sawyer Island (opposite).

Tomorrowland. It was all vending machines, and the operation would take in many thousands of dollars every day in coin. We just couldn't keep up with the count, so we worked up a formula where we weighed the coins and used that weight as a basis for our deposits."

But sometimes all those deposits could not cover the expenses of operating the Park. Just one month after the Park opened, Mother Nature seemed bound and determined to dry up what little cash Walt had and test his perseverance one more time.

Fifteen days of 100-degree weather combined with 90 percent humidity to drive attendance down to a trickle. Walt was seen out in front of the Golden Horseshoe wondering aloud if the paying public would ever come back again. When the weekly paychecks were issued, members of the management team were told not to cash theirs until they were certain that all of the hourly employees' checks were covered by the dwindling bank funds.

The opening of Disneyland may have captured the attention of the nation, but the nation's press found it far from glittering with pixie dust. Incomplete guest services, operational chaos, and the seemingly endless miscues during those early days tested the nerves and patience of nearly everyone. While Walt busied himself fixing the problems, the nation's press did nothing but complain.

Apparently unaware of the plumber's strike that had threatened the Park's very opening, one paper observed, "There was a cunning lack of drinking fountains, fueling one's thirst for shelling out more money for soda drinks." A headline warned of "The $17 Million Dollar People Trap that Mickey Mouse built." Still another declared, "Walt's dream is a nightmare," and then attacked: "I attended the so-called press premiere of Disneyland, a fiasco the like of which I cannot recall in thirty years of show life. To me, it felt like a giant cash register, clicking and clanging, as creatures of Disney magic came tumbling down from their lofty places in my daydreams to peddle and perish their charms with the aggressiveness of so many curbside barkers. With this harsh stroke, he transforms a beautiful dream into a blatant nightmare."

As the Disneyland press reviews began to come in, the beleaguered Disney no doubt would have enjoyed the reassurance of Theodore Roosevelt, who once said, "It is not the critic who counts, not the man who points out how the strong man stumbled or where the doer of deeds could have done better. The credit belongs to the man who is actually in the arena, whose face is marred by dust and sweat and blood."

Walt Disney took special pride in keeping in touch with Disneyland guests of all ages.

Although Disney had developed a tough hide from the sting of past critics, he was frustrated by the lack of appreciation for his struggling young
park. A United Press writer cornered him on a second trip to see if any changes
had been made. He discovered more drinking fountains and all but one of the
attractions finally in working order. But then he asked about the Park's prices,
and he touched off a Walt Disney who was finally tiring of the "commercial"
rap.

"We have to charge what we do because this Park cost a lot to build and
maintain. I have no government subsidy. The public is my subsidy," Disney
argued.

"I mortgaged everything I own and put it in jeopardy for this Park.
Commercial? How have I stayed in business all my life? The critics must know
a newspaper exists on advertising. They're crazy!

"We have a lot of free things in the Park. No other place has as high a quality. I stand here in the Park and talk to people. It's a most gratifying thing. All I've got from the public is thank-yous."

GROWING PAINS

In fact, no one was more sensitive or sympathetic to the needs of that paying public than Walt Disney himself. During the first year he made countless trips to the Park, calling for lengthy and intense walk-throughs with his key personnel. "I always keep a practical eye towards its appeal to the public," he said.

One major problem that quickly became apparent involved the public directly. Visitors to Disneyland that first year paid the main-gate admission to the Park and then found that each attraction had its own ticket booth. Before long, asking the guests to put their hands in their money pockets each time they came to a new attraction had turned into a psychologically bad situation. To many, it seemed like a slow death by the old Chinese water torture, with clinking coins replacing the dripping water.

Soon, perhaps the most creative ticket system of all time was put into use. The most popular attractions, like the Jungle Cruise and the *Mark Twain*, were plagued with long lines of waiting guests. Disneyland officials were perplexed by their inability to get the crowds to try out the smaller attractions, which had short or no lines.

This problem led to the creation of the famous Disneyland ticket book. The books rated the attractions from least expensive, "A," to most expensive, "C," and they contained several tickets from each category. Once the guests started finding these A and B tickets in their pockets—having already paid for them up front—they were more willing to investigate the smaller attractions. The guests finally began to disperse evenly across the Park, and, as a bonus, they discovered the real "sleepers" they probably would have otherwise missed.

The idea worked brilliantly, far beyond anyone's fondest expectations. The ticket-book concept grew dramatically in popularity during the years ahead. For many young Disneyland fans, the lettered coupons became their first standard for bartering in their neighborhoods as they saved and traded their coupons from past visits, the way earlier generations had collected baseball cards.

Over the years, as new Disneyland attractions became bigger and more

The big "Mooseketeer" Roy Williams (below), *who cohosted television's "The Mickey Mouse Club" with Jimmie Dodd, often could be found sketching for guests at Disneyland during the Park's early years.*

Early growing pains led to a backstage infrastructure to house a steadily increasing number of special entertainment parade floats and displays (opposite).

sophisticated, the C tickets were joined by the Ds and later by the Es. Soon, the E ticket came to stand for the best, most exciting, and most thrilling adventures in the Park.

Astronaut Sally Ride gave perhaps the greatest tribute to the Disneyland ticket book. Her first words to the press and to the world after ascending into space aboard the Space Shuttle were, "That's a real E ticket ride!" America knew exactly what she meant.

Another of the early problems that Walt ran up against ironically related to the outside staff that he had hired to provide many of the park services in which his own people lacked expertise. Richard Nunis was a training supervisor at the time. "Walt didn't have an experienced staff at the beginning," Nunis remembers. "He tried to go out and get the best experts in things we knew nothing about. We had outside operators for the parking lot, security, custodial, and even for crowd control." At that time, Nunis points out, the food and merchandise people were employed by the lessees who signed operating contracts that had provided Disney with much-needed cash.

From the way the crowd control employees yelled at the customers, it appeared that they assumed their mission to be cattle-herding. They lasted only one day, according to Nunis. The custodial company's standards apparently stopped at cursory cleanliness. The security guards evidently thought that they had been retained specifically to protect Disney property from thugs, a description they liberally applied to anyone who came through the gate.

"It was a disaster," Nunis concluded. "The only employees who really worked out well were the attraction operators. That's because we hired and trained them ourselves. The others just didn't understand what Walt really wanted."

What Walt really wanted were employees with a ready smile and a knack for dealing pleasantly with large numbers of people. He quickly replaced most of the outsiders with more of his own staff and trained them in his own "Disney University." An entirely new vocabulary was created that overturned traditional amusement park lingo. Paying customers became "guests," each and every one to be treated as a VIP. Employees were dubbed "hosts" and "hostesses," and all the members of the entire Disneyland organization, from Walt Disney to the newest employee, were to be addressed by their first names to ensure a casual, relaxed, and friendly atmosphere. Public areas were referred to as "on stage," behind the scenes as "backstage." Even the time-honored amusement park "ride" disappeared, replaced by "attraction" or "adventure,"

Walt takes a moment to review the Park's guidebook in 1957. He concerned himself with every detail, no matter how minor, of his Magic Kingdom.

after guests had announced that they wanted to go on the *Mark Twain* or the Jungle Cruise, but they didn't want to go on the rides (evidently a very negative amusement park connotation). The graduates of the Disney University quickly fulfilled the standards of excellence for service that Walt Disney set for them.

Part of the service Walt expected from his attraction operators was to keep guests relaxed while waiting in line by diverting them with a line of banter that went well beyond the official information narrations. This was the single greatest step toward establishing the world-famous Disneyland "personality," and the new coupon books even made the job easier.

Jungle Cruise operators became masters of alliteration. "Please tear an E coupon from your ticket book . . . that's 'E' as in Euripides, 'E' as in extremely excited, eggplant-eating, egotistical elephant. Please hand it to the tall, tan, ticket-taking ticket-taker, taking tickets at the twisting, turning turnstile."

Others found different ways to keep long lines of guests distracted from their tedious wait. "All right, everybody listen up!" the ticket-taker in the line would say. "Everyone now . . . stomp your left foot once. Now stomp your right foot. Thank you very much. One of our snakes got away this morning, but I'm sure that took care of him!"

Walt and his daughter Sharon visit with guests in Adventureland in August 1957. Walt often took the time to see Disneyland as the guests saw it.

Ludicrous? Of course, but cheerful "tall, tan ticket-takers" with wacky personalities worked wonders on groups of tired guests with nothing to do but wait in line.

DISNEYLAND—THE LABORATORY

Throughout the early days, Disneyland was, more than anything else, a laboratory for Walt. "I watch every bit of a big crowd," Walt said, "and find out where we need to improve our crowd control conditions to make it easier to get around, and our shade areas and all the problems we have in the summer."

He wouldn't let the landscapers fence in the lawns until he first saw where the guests wanted to go. If they often cut across particular grass areas, then he read it as a signal that sidewalks needed to be poured in that section.

It was a continual process, learning from the public—its needs, its desires, its interests—and it took Walt to Disneyland for many walk-throughs. These often took place late in the day, causing him to remain at the Park overnight in his Main Street apartment located over the Fire House. More than once, he was awakened at dawn by the sound of jackhammers. In an instant,

The rarely seen interior of Walt's private apartment, located directly above the Fire Station at City Hall on Main Street, where Walt often spent the night.

he was up and out on the street, talking to the workmen, to grasp the problem at hand and toss it back to his engineers and designers to solve on the double.

Walt also expected his designers to go to Disneyland as often as possible. He wanted them to check the attractions they had worked on. "He required that we walk through the front gate," said John Hench, "and stand in line with the guests, to listen and watch . . . to see how they reacted. I don't know of any other design firm that's ever had this privilege."

Disney himself spent a great deal of time on the attractions, not only checking them but also monitoring the performance levels of his own staff, a task he performed rigorously. Dick Nunis, who by now had become responsible for managing Adventureland, got a "battle scar" from Disney. "Walt came running down to the Jungle Cruise, got on a boat and took a trip, returning with both eyebrows raised." (His eyebrows were a Disney barometer—one raised was bad, two raised meant deep trouble.)

"What's the trip time supposed to be?" asked Disney.

"Well, sir, it's seven minutes," replied Nunis.

"I just had a four-and-a-half-minute trip and went through the hippo pool so fast, I couldn't tell if they were hippos or rhinos! How would you feel if you paid to go to the movies and they cut the center reel out of the picture?"

For the next three weeks, Nunis spent so much time on the jungle boats training the crew that he almost became seasick. Then Disney arrived again, riding the first boat, then the second, and so on, through the last available boat. He was determined that Nunis would not "stack the deck" with his best speaker on the first boat (a ploy that Nunis admits he had tried). On each ride, the timing of the trip was perfect. After this experience, everyone realized that Disney was very serious about giving the guests the best show possible.

The ride operators, however, were not the only ones to run afoul of his standards. Nearby, a young publicist named Marty Sklar had parked his car too close to the Frontierland river. The trees and vegetation were so sparse that the car was clearly visible to the *Mark Twain* as it passed by. And visible to Disney, who came running up in a floppy hat, waving his arms. "What are you doing here in 1860 with a 1955 automobile?" he snapped.

All such "Walt battle scars" represented lessons that had been learned, and they became badges for future success. Today, both Nunis and Sklar are top-ranking Disney executives.

The Disneyland laboratory often provided data unrelated to the guest experience but that proved positively startling to the Park's hardware suppliers. One ride system, for example, used a power supply provided by the same kind of batteries as those used on forklifts. The batteries were guaranteed for one year, and, as one might suspect, the salesman returned a few days after the expiration of the warranty, expecting to write another large order. The batteries, however, still operated perfectly. He returned the following year, only to face the same situation. Finally, the battery company engineers were dispatched to the Park to find out why their "one-year battery" was performing so extraordinarily well. After much investigation, they concluded that Disneyland used the batteries far more than expected, and fully discharged the battery each day. This full discharge and recharge cycle dramatically extended the life of the one-year batteries fivefold.

Other manufacturers were equally surprised by the data they gathered in the Park's "real-people" lab. "Lifetime" carpets gave way in a few months to the crush of daily crowds, as did linoleum, and even heavy-duty concrete. Roofings, street pavings, paint, and other finishes were torture-tested by the severe daily wash-downs required to meet the Park's immaculate cleanliness standards. Literally hundreds of other items were subjected to real-life durability tests that provided more useful data than the most comprehensive lab tests that the manufacturers could devise themselves.

VANISHING ACTS

It has often been said the only bad publicity is no publicity. Despite the bad press, the public showed up at the main gate in ever-increasing numbers. But guests also discovered a few causes for complaint, some of them related to the attractions themselves. Ever-sensitive to the guest response, Disney changed anything that failed to meet the public's needs, usually replacing it with a better idea.

One of the first changes came on the Disneyland railroad. While the guests clamored to get aboard the passenger train, almost all rejected the freight train. They especially resented being put into the cattle cars, and on more than one occasion, guests could be heard "bellowing" like protesting animals as they were "herded" into the cars. The freight train was quickly remodeled as an additional passenger train.

Rivaling the cattle cars for guest dissatisfaction that first year was the Fantasyland boat ride, known at that time as the "Canal Boats of the World," and affectionately known by Dick Nunis as "The Mud Bank Ride." It was intended to be a journey past miniature re-creations of the great landmarks of the world, but time and money problems prevented its completion. At open-

Designer Wathel Rogers creates a miniature house for Storybook Land in 1956. Rogers later used his mechanical skills to help pioneer Disney's revolutionary Audio-Animatronics *system of animation.*

ing, the boats cruised past barren shores. It soon became a standard joke among Fantasyland employees: "The miniature landscaping is so miniature, you can't see it!" One of the first operators remembers the embarrassment. "There was nothing there, only weeds. The enclosed outboard motors that powered the little canal boats were always overheating, so we'd often have to pull boats filled with guests around by hand, sort of like the 'Volga boatmen.' There was no set spiel, because there was nothing to talk about, and anyway, we couldn't be heard over the roar of the outboard motors, in the unlikely event they kept running."

It took almost a year to transform the Canal Boats of the World into the kind of attraction Walt had originally planned. His early concept, for a "Lilliputian" village populated with miniature animated figures, had proven unworkable. The technology did not yet exist that could bring to life the imposing giant and the diminutive figures that Walt wanted to inhabit his village. So "Lilliputian Land" begat "Storybook Land"—where guests would ride those same Canal Boats past exquisite miniature scenes from Walt's classic animated films. Each scene was carefully landscaped with tiny trees and

Guests sail through Storybook Land (below), *an exquisite land of fairytale miniatures once inhabited by "worker giants"* (opposite).

shrubs, all living, all trained to retain the diminishing scale perfectly. It re-opened to enthusiastic reviews, and, while remaining virtually unchanged, it continues to be a favorite of the guests.

Unfortunately, however, some things just could not be fixed. For example, the "Phantom Boats," which debuted at the Tomorrowland lagoon short-ly after the grand opening of Disneyland, promptly established a reputation for unreliability that exceeded even that of the Canal Boats. To begin with, the ugly, finned little vessels looked as if they had been intended for Batman. More important, each boat that left the dock seemed to have only a fifty-fifty chance of making it back without having to be towed. After circling around the lagoon for two summers, the Phantom Boats finally lived up to their name and vanished from the Park.

Other elements of Disneyland would soon vanish as well. One, in par-ticular, had four legs and worked primarily in Frontierland. "We were loading a stagecoach one time," remembered a longtime driver, "when we looked up and people were hollerin' and yellin' from the *Mark Twain*, pointing at an-

In the Park's early days, Art Linkletter and his wife, Lois, gamely try out the Phantom Boats, a chancy excursion given the vessel's spotty record for returning to the home dock. Fortunately for everyone, the Phantom Boats vanished a short while later.

other stagecoach with four ponies on the dead run—and no driver. They ran into a coach that was loading and turned it clean over on its side."

The driver had a lot of other war stories from the Disneyland Pony Farm. Walt soon realized that his beloved horses and mules, so carefully raised and trained by Owen Pope, still behaved unpredictably in public. "Another time," the driver continued, "a shot of steam from the train scared the ponies at Rainbow Ridge, in the Frontierland Painted Desert. A safety device malfunctioned, releasing the coach from the front wheels, and it turned over with seventeen people on board. The ponies panicked and they raced along the rest of the trail and came home dragging the two front wheels." After several other mishaps in which guests narrowly escaped injury, a regretful Walt was convinced by Joe Fowler that the stagecoaches were an idea whose time had passed, and in 1959 they closed forever.

The Disneyland Stage Coach makes its way through the Painted Desert.

Perhaps the strangest four-legged sight of all came when one of the huge Belgian horses, which weighed up to 2,200 pounds, bolted from the streetcar it was pulling along Main Street and ran away. As the horse went clopping down the street, the drawbar fell and hit the animal's heels. It ran for nearly twenty yards, down to the end of Main Street, until, trying to make the sharp turn into the Town Square, it slipped and fell with a thunderous crash. Unlike the stagecoaches, though, the horse-drawn streetcars were given a reprieve, and remain to this day.

No animals in the Disneyland Pony Farm were more difficult to work with than the Frontierland "Pack Mules." They began their show business careers by nibbling at guests' souvenir hats as they saddled up. When the operators got wise and started collecting the hats before loading, the mules occasionally retaliated by nipping shoes. One mule mistook a girl's long blonde ponytail for a "hay snack."

Most embarrassing, though, was the mule's work ethic. Although blessed with extraordinarily short work hours, the mules would stop for no apparent reason along the trail and refuse to continue, regardless of the verbal lashings applied by the mule skinner. And almost anywhere, at any time, one of the creatures would break into a loud and repetitious series of brayings that sounded astonishingly like "hee haw."

It was a tribute to Walt's patience and love for animals that the Pack Mules weren't sent packing. They would remain at Disneyland, cantankerous personalities and all, until retiring in 1973 to make way for a major Frontierland expansion.

Occasional mishaps along the stagecoach route (opposite) *eventually brought an end to the line. The unpredictable Pack Mules, taking on a new load of young pioneers* (below), *caused different kinds of problems.*

THE BIG TOP'S BIG FLOP

Walt Disney was directly responsible for one of the big Disneyland flops. He had always loved a good circus. The work his animators put into the cartoon classic *Dumbo* remains to this day perhaps the most imaginative animation ever created. For everyone at the Disney Studio, it was a work of love. Years later, however, Dumbo's terrifying drunken nightmare, "Pink Elephants on Parade," came to life for almost everyone when the circus came to Disneyland.

Walt wanted a circus—"The Mickey Mouse Club Circus"—to run for six weeks starting at Christmastime. The idea met with downright opposition by some of his staff. "Walt, you just can't do this!" said C. V. Wood, one of his key administrators. "A circus always plays by itself. The guy comes to Disneyland to stay around for four hours and see what you've got. He's not going to spend two of those hours at a damn circus!"

Disney was undaunted. In order to gain more support for the idea, he decided that the Studio would eventually make a film called *Toby Tyler or Ten Weeks with a Circus*. He then convinced his brother Roy that they would need the huge circus tent and the old wagons he had located. As one might suspect, all of these items found their way down to Disneyland.

Joe Fowler remembered opening night as if it were a recurring nightmare. "Walt and I were sitting together. The first thing that happened, Owen Pope brought his big pumpkin chariot into the huge circus tent pulled by six of his most beautiful ponies. One of the wheels caught a large diagonal post that held the big top up and carried it away. I thought, 'Oh, no, my God, no!' But fortunately the tent still held up."

According to Fowler, that was only the beginning, as things got worse. One of his staff came running up and said, "Joe, the llamas have escaped!" Excusing himself from Walt, Fowler and his staff chased the llamas along the railroad track, finally recapturing them at the Main Street Station. When he returned, Walt told him, "Well, Joe, you missed the best part of the show. One of the leading ladies bent down and split her tights!"

The troubles continued to mount. The circus people were a tough lot used to drinking and gambling between shows. During the premiere of the circus parade, a black panther grabbed the paw of a neighboring tiger and chewed it off. The biggest problem, however, came from the public, which just didn't seem to want to see the circus, regardless of adjustments in schedules, ticket prices, or anything else.

A concept sketch sets out the short-lived Mickey Mouse Club Circus, the first and biggest flop in Disneyland history.

"That was the first time that we learned this lesson," concludes Joe Fowler. "People came to Disneyland to see Disneyland." The big top became the Park's biggest flop. (Three decades would pass before it would return for another try, in a new, different form.)

THE DELUGE

With the help of his staff, Disney finally ironed out the kinks in his new park. He then turned his attention to expanding its potential. His number-one priority during the first year of operation was playing "catch-up," to increase the Park's limited ride capacity. During the first twelve months, the number of attractions was more than doubled. "As long as there is imagination left in the world," Walt said, "Disneyland will never be completed."

One major addition Walt considered essential was an aerial tramway to run between Fantasyland and Tomorrowland, which, he was convinced, would provide a spectacular view of Disneyland. Having heard about a suitable system in Europe, he dispatched Joe Fowler on a mission to get hold of it.

SKYRIDE IN FANTASYLAND

Realizing that the view above Disneyland is pretty spectacular (shown opposite, below *in 1966), Walt Disney had his artists sketch out a concept* (opposite, above) *for his skyway, and he proudly dedicated it in 1956* (below).

Fowler returned on the weekend of the first rain of the rainy season, in January 1956. No ordinary rain, it fell into the category known as a real "frog-choker." Walt had come to the Park with Dick Irvine, using not the incomplete freeway but the surface streets, still the insider's most efficient approach to the Park. But they, too, became flooded. "That's okay," Walt said. "We'll just spend the weekend right here if we have to."

They had to. After "testing Walt" during the summer with record heat waves, it seemed that Mother Nature was now going to re-create the great flood. She provided a record rain that tested and surpassed the total water circulation system of the entire park. The Canal Boats of the World overflowed. The Rivers of America overflowed. Fowler remembers a record-setting seven inches of rain, in a Southern California area that most people think of as a desert. But the weekend served an important purpose, as it gave Disney, Fowler, and Irvine the time together to finalize the plans for the Alpine tramway across Disneyland. It would join several other major additions as part of the Park's first important growth program.

EXPANDING THE FRONTIER

The first summer, the *Mark Twain* not only ruled as "Queen of the River," she was, in fact, the sole floating constituent of the Rivers of America. By the Christmas holidays, the nationwide Davy Crockett craze was in full swing. To take advantage of Davy's sudden popularity, Walt had a special present readied for the Park—the two keelboats actually used in the filming of "Davy Crockett's Keelboat Race," an episode of Disney's weekly television show. Davy's *Bertha Mae* and Mike Fink's *Gullywhumper* were specially modified to carry guests down the river. Ron Dominguez less than fondly remembers playing the role of Mike Fink, always having to "lose" his jousting contests with hero Davy Crockett by being knocked off his keelboat into the chilly river.

Soon, the river became host to even more water traffic. Indian War Canoes began "guest-powered" trips around the river while log rafts opened a ferry service to Tom Sawyer Island, where a series of caves, bridges, tunnels, forts, treehouses, and fishing docks made it an incredibly popular "kid's place."

One of the biggest kids of all was Walt Disney himself, who would often take a pole and fish from the dock with the other youngsters. One day, after fishing for some time without so much as a nibble, Disney turned to the dock attendant and said, "There's no fish in the river!" The attendant was caught a

The Mike Fink Keelboats have plied the Rivers of America in Frontierland since December 1955. The original boats actually appeared in "Davy Crockett's Keelboat Race," a special episode of Walt's weekly television show.

bit off guard but quickly recovered. "There's fish there, all right, but the water's so muddy, they can't even see the bait." Walt thought for a minute and then replied, "Well, I fished the Missouri River and it was a lot muddier than this, but the fish sure saw the bait!"

Explorers like Davy Crockett weren't the only Frontierland settlers to make their homes at the Park. Real, live Indians set up camp during the first summer in a tiny village, then migrated the next year to a more spacious village along the shores of the Rivers of America. Guests visiting the Indian Village were invited to take part in authentic ceremonial dances and could purchase handmade souvenirs at the Indian Trading Post.

Disney's last and most complex addition to Frontierland that first year

The early years of Frontierland offered a variety of pleasures. Guest-powered canoes and steam-powered stern-wheelers make up part of the water traffic on the Rivers of America (left). Young explorers watch a traditional Indian ceremony at the Frontierland "Indian Village" (opposite, below, left), located where Bear Country is today. Teetering rock columns along Nature's Wonderland were designed to startle guests and add the element of danger (opposite, below, right). Old Unfaithful Geyser blows its top in the Painted Desert in Nature's Wonderland (below). Changing winds and slow mine trains sometimes combined forces to give guests unscheduled showers. The Painted Desert in Nature's Wonderland also featured the bubbling Devil's Paint Pots (above).

Designer Marc Davis always sketched the first and last frames of animation for each scene. These are two scenes from Nature's Wonderland.

was inspired by his Academy Award–winning film *The Living Desert*. The "Rainbow Caverns Mine Train" took guests across a cactus-studded wasteland that re-created the great open spaces of the American southwest. For the actual Rainbow Caverns, he turned once again to his top animation background artist, Claude Coats, for a little studio magic. Disney had found out about fluorescent dyes that, when added to waterfalls, became brilliantly illuminated through the same "black light" that was used in the Fantasyland dark rides.

Coats experimented with all six rainbow colors falling side by side in one big wide waterfall. "Each color was in a separate trough," he said, "but as they hit the bottom, we needed to get them as close together as possible to be believable. But a mathematician who was working at the Studio on another project told us that it was statistically impossible, that the splash between the colors couldn't be controlled. He said the whole thing would be gray within a week." Coats reported this bleak observation to Disney and was treated to one raised eyebrow. "Well, Claude, it's kind of fun to do the impossible, isn't it?" Disney left Coats with the problem, and, after weeks of experimenting, Coats, working with John Hench, left Disney with a solution: an ingenious entanglement of hairlike fibrous material that reduced splashing to nearly nothing.

"With the opening of Rainbow Caverns," the press release said, "Walt Disney has brought to a close his Magic Wonderland's first major expansion program only days from the completion of the Park's first year. The program fulfills Walt's promise for this summer season of 'More room, more rides for fun.'"

Walt reviews the progress of Fort Wilderness on Tom Sawyer Island in 1956.

CHAPTER FOUR

Growing Up

The way I see it, Disneyland will never be finished.
It's something we can keep developing and adding to.
A motion picture is different. Once it's wrapped up
and sent out for processing, we're through with it.
If there are things that could be improved, we can't
do them anymore. I've always wanted to work on
something alive, something that keeps growing.
We've got that at Disneyland.

WALT DISNEY

DISNEYLAND - U.S.A.

At the end of that first year, the in-fant Disneyland finally got up on wobbly legs and learned to walk. Once it was secure, however, it did not stop growing. The subsequent decade brought a great many improvements and changes, as Disney continued to experiment with his living laboratory.

CATS

Ken Anderson remembers the time when Walt discovered an empty space at Disneyland. (Empty spaces were always anathema to Disney.) It was inside Sleeping Beauty Castle at the entrance to Fantasyland, and it would soon turn out to be less empty than Walt had thought.

Disney invited Anderson and *20,000 Leagues* set designer Emile Kuri on a walk-through of the facility. Anderson had just finished his work on *Sleeping Beauty*, one of the Studio's most ambitious and beautiful animated films. The trio ascended an obscure ladder high inside the castle, and Walt continued to talk to Anderson. "Now, Ken, I know this is awfully crowded, but I'm sure you can build a Sleeping Beauty attraction right in here . . . in this castle."

Meanwhile, Kuri, dressed in an immaculate white suit, had moved ahead of the group and was poking curiously around the premises. It seemed that everywhere he poked, he discovered cats. There were cats on the beams, cats on the walkways, and cats underfoot with practically every step. And they were wild, not friendly in the least. It seemed that they had probably taken up residence in the castle sometime during the construction period two years earlier.

Kuri jumped over a partition to a spot where a large cardboard box rested with a gunnysack over it. In the dim light, he picked up the old gunnysack. Suddenly, shockingly, his sparkling white suit turned gray. He let out a half-scream, half-cry for help and began jumping up and down violently. In des-peration, he ran toward Disney and Anderson.

"We were covered with fleas," remembers Anderson. "It seemed the whole area was so filled with cat fleas that they were happy to see people! We were slapping ourselves and rolling up our trousers when Walt said, 'Don't worry, fellows. I've got a phone here!' Disney made a quick call and said, 'Hel-lo, this is Walt.' There was a pause. 'Walt Disney, that's who!'"

The Grand Canyon Diorama (above) and the Columbia *sailing
ship—the "gem of the ocean"—*(right) *joined the Disneyland list of
attractions in 1958.*

The Clock of the World *welcomes guests into early Tomorrowland
(below). The Clock told the time of day, right down to the minute,
anywhere on the planet Earth.*

After the great escape, and the even greater de-fleaing, Disney wouldn't let the staff harm the cats. After all, an entire "civilization" had taken up permanent residence in the formerly lifeless castle. He arranged for their relocation, finding new families for the "castle cats."

By the way, Anderson did indeed figure out a way to cram a Sleeping Beauty attraction inside a castle that was never planned to host a show. When the attraction opened in 1957, the guests climbed a winding staircase through the castle, where beautiful miniature dioramas unfolded before them, telling the story of Sleeping Beauty. Irvine thought of the dioramas as being like department-store window dressing, but he gave Anderson high marks for "great illusions and beautiful sketches."

THE WORLD'S LONGEST DIORAMA

"It took the creative imagination of Walt Disney, and his artisans more than 80,000 man-hours of design, painting, and construction, to complete the first 'reproduction' of Arizona's famed Grand Canyon," proclaimed a 1958 Disneyland press release.

Not content to let his steam trains simply function as a transportation system around the Park, Walt was determined to create some sort of show that would involve the trains themselves. Hence, the arrival of the "Grand Canyon Diorama," a Disneyland manifestation of the future Academy Award–winning film *Grand Canyon*, which was being shot in Arizona and edited to the music of Ferde Grofé's "Grand Canyon Suite."

The diorama, the longest in the world, measured 306 feet wide by 34 feet high. It had consumed 300 gallons of paint and 14 palette colors applied to a seamless, hand-woven canvas prepared especially for the Park. The diorama was housed in a long wooden shack that enveloped the entire railroad track between Tomorrowland and Main Street. As the guests pulled out of Tomorrowland Station, they entered a dark tunnel and emerged to view the breathtaking scenes of the Grand Canyon. A wide variety of animals native to the region (real . . . but stuffed) were displayed in settings that represented the most colorful events of a typical day: sunrise, a midafternoon thundershower, and sunset.

For the occasion of the steam train's first trip through the Grand Canyon Diorama, Walt Disney was joined by Fred Gurley, chairman of Santa Fe Railroad's board of directors. Adding particular resonance to the ceremonies was the presence of Chief Nevangnewa, a ninety-six-year-old Hopi Indian. Disney

The Flight Circle in Tomorrowland was the home of high-flying model airplanes. The 76-foot-tall TWA Rocket to the Moon looms in the background.

had, at long last, brought a special significance to the railroad that had first chugged its way around his backyard so many years before.

GEM OF THE OCEAN

Regardless of all the canoes, rafts, and keelboats that plied the Rivers of America, Disney wanted a second large ship at Disneyland . . . a sailing ship . . . one with some real history behind it. He had Admiral Joe Fowler examine every maritime museum in the country. Fowler concluded that the perfect ship to reproduce had been built in Massachusetts in 1787 and was the first American sailing ship to go around the world. It was the *Columbia*.

The sailing ship *Columbia* seemed to be exactly what Disney had in mind, so Fowler was commissioned to build an exact but scaled-down replica of the original. Disney became totally fascinated by the process of its construction. Fowler told him that it was customary when building the old sailing ships to put a silver dollar under each mast for good luck before it was set. Disney personally put a dollar under each of the three masts of the *Columbia*. When it came time to christen the ship, Disney assigned his ever-popular Mouseketeers to be the uniformed crew, and he had Admiral Fowler deck himself out in a skipper's outfit of the 1700s. The *Columbia* also carried ten cannon, as did the original, and it was acknowledged as the first three-masted windjammer to be built in the United States in more than one hundred years.

YESTERDAYLAND

Perhaps Walt's most frustrating task involved keeping the "tomorrow"

Skyway buckets pass through the icebound grottoes of the Matterhorn, while tandem bobsleds streak across rock bridges (opposite). *The buckets and bobsleds were exchanged for different models in later years, as evidenced in the late-model Matterhorn bobsled entering a splashdown* (below).

in Tomorrowland. At best a compromise that had been miraculously pulled off for the Park's grand premiere, the area offered only two attractions with any claim to tomorrow, the Autopia freeway and the Rocket to the Moon. Its other attractions, the 20,000 Leagues Under the Sea exhibit, Circarama, the "Flight Circle" (a demonstration area for flying model aircraft), were hardly the "right stuff" to lead the way into the future.

With time and money running short before the opening of Tomorrowland, Walt had been forced to accept several corporate county-fair-type exhibits to populate the buildings. The Monsanto "Hall of Chemistry," the Dutch Boy Paint "Color Gallery," and Kaiser's "Hall of Aluminum Fame" did little more than promote the companies themselves, and even less to promote the future.

Then, in 1957, came the "Viewliner," the first future-oriented transportation system to be unleashed on the Tomorrowland area. A slick, well-proportioned train of the 1950s, it bore a striking resemblance to the Buck Rogers spaceships that graced the pages of the Sunday comics. It also adapted the best futuristic designs of the day and used one of the most reliable power systems that the transportation world could muster at the time. The power

plant was an Oldsmobile V-8 "Rocket" engine, and the dashboard was a transplant of a 1955 Olds "88" instrument panel. As the Viewliner rambled around the Tomorrowland area, however, it became clear that it did not live up to the future that Walt had in mind.

THE HIGHWAY IN THE SKY

In Cologne, Germany, Joe Fowler and Roger Broggie had seen the real future: a working monorail system that had been developed by the Alweg Corporation. They reported back to Walt that it probably could be built and operated successfully at Disneyland. Broggie soon found an interesting and delicate balancing act occurring. "It was between engineering people who wanted to go in a straight line forever with no grades, and the Disney art directors who wanted to draw tight turning radii and plot an interesting ride that climbed maximum grades in order to thrill the guests." As one might suspect, the pragmatics of simple design gave way to the more complicated show layouts.

Walt wanted to debut his new monorail in the summer of 1959, less than a year away. After a meeting with the German engineers, the decision was made to build the vehicles in California, thus saving precious time that would otherwise be taken by shipping the equipment all the way from Germany. Ironically, it was seeing the Viewliner in operation that convinced the German engineers of Disney's manufacturing skills.

Disney saw the monorail system as a sleek, all-electric "Highway in the Sky" that would weave together the most ambitious expansion program in the Park's young history. It would wind around the Tomorrowland area on a sce-

A passing of eras—the 1957 Viewliner passes by the Santa Fe & Disneyland Railroad on the outskirts of Tomorrowland (opposite). The streamlined Viewliner would soon pass into history, to be replaced by the even sleeker Monorail in 1959.

nic journey that included a cruise over the new Submarine Lagoon (the former home of the short-lived Phantom Boats) and around a new landmark for Orange County, Matterhorn Mountain.

"MEN TO MATCH MY MOUNTAIN"

One day, an employee from the Disney Studio was visiting the Park and found Walt sitting on a bench between Fantasyland and Tomorrowland, sort of staring off into space. "What are you looking at, Walt?" she asked. "My mountain," was the response.

On a trip to Switzerland in 1958, Disney had become fascinated by the dominating, angular peak that sits on the Swiss-Italian border. The Matterhorn had not been conquered until 1865, and even then it had claimed the lives of more than half the climbing party. But Walt had just conquered the summit via his 1959 feature film *Third Man on the Mountain*. And he was determined to bring the Matterhorn home with him—home to Disneyland.

The Disneyland version of the Matterhorn was scaled down to 1/100 of the original, resulting in a 147-foot summit that would tower above the Fantasyland castle. The Matterhorn would become Disneyland's first classic "thrill ride," as guests boarded four-person bobsleds for a high-speed, twisting, turbulent journey down its slopes.

Joe Fowler was especially concerned about the safety of the bobsleds as they careened down the mountain. He found a water ride in a park outside of London where the vehicles were slowed by landing in a pool of water. The adaptation at Disneyland resulted in the famous "bobsled splashdown," which would become one of the most photographed scenes in the Park.

Fowler had faced some construction challenges before, but building a mountain with five hundred tons of steel, with no two pieces the same length, proved particularly exasperating. Equally challenging, though, was the task put before Bill Evans's landscape group. For probably the first time in history, landscapers found themselves called upon to determine just what would constitute a "timberline" on a fourteen-story building. Evans finally concluded that it would be about halfway up the summit, between sixty-five and seventy-five feet up the Matterhorn's slopes. He then applied the same sense of forced perspective that Disney's architects had used in many parts of the Park. At the higher elevations, Evans's staff dangled precariously from cranes as they planted stunted spruce trees, while, at the base, full-grown trees rose above thousands of flowers.

A guest finds a quiet spot in Tomorrowland.

As construction neared completion, it was time to test the bobsleds that wound their way through the mountain. During the test runs, Disney saw bobsled after bobsled careen down the mountain with their passengers represented in the form of four sandbags. When the bobsleds were ready for a live test pilot, Disney selected the ride's designer, Vic Greene, for the honor of the first run, accompanied, naturally, by three sandbags. Greene survived, and the most unusual roller coaster in the world was now complete.

THE VOYAGE THROUGH LIQUID SPACE

With its next great attraction, Tomorrowland went from the heights to the depths. Dick Irvine talked to Disney about a glass-bottom boat to cruise

The "world of liquid space," drained for renovations, is prepared for Submarine voyagers.

over a picturesque lagoon in Tomorrowland. The guests would see underwater life and a live show, not unlike Florida's famous Cypress Gardens. But Disney's response took the idea two steps further. "No, let's do a real submarine ride. Let's take them down and give them ports to look out of."

The journey beneath the oceans would be partly real and partly an illusion. The guests would board the submarines and be seated well below the water level, their view through "liquid space" provided by individual portholes. Outside the submarines were amazing coral gardens, whales, sharks . . . and even mermaids. As the submarines continued their journey, they would "descend" beneath the North Pole. Great turbulence could be seen outside the portholes, but the submarines would never actually descend any lower than they were at the start of the ride.

As the design and layout progressed, it became clear that the submarines would not be able simply to cruise through the outdoor lagoon. The mechan-

Vice-President and Mrs. Richard M. Nixon and their daughters, Julie and Tricia, were on hand with Walt Disney and "pilot" Art Linkletter (opposite) *to dedicate the Monorail on June 14, 1959.*

ics of the animated creatures and the requirements for controlled lighting called for a large, separate show building. But such a huge "concrete box" would be a real eyesore sitting in the middle of Tomorrowland, and besides, the Autopia was already taking up all the available space.

Bill Evans was called in to provide the solution. After a great deal of give and take with the engineers, he convinced them to design the "concrete box" to carry a heavy load of topsoil—and support the winding roadways of the Autopia. "We literally landscaped the roof," remembers Evans. "We designed it to look like a naturally woodsy scene that actually enhanced the Autopia. Today, the guest looking out across the Submarine Lagoon sees a rather substantial forest. He has no idea that there's a huge 'parking garage' underneath that forest, a great big space filled with sea serpents, giant squid, whales, and lost ships in the sunken city of Atlantis."

Early on, the United States Navy expressed an interest in becoming involved in the project, but retired Admiral Joe Fowler recommended against it. His thirty-two years in the navy had taught him that Disney would be so hamstrung with orders and regulations that the ride probably would never get completed.

It is with some degree of irony, however, that Fowler remembers several top-ranking naval officers coming out to the Park to ride the subs. As they left the dock, Fowler put his most polite foot forward. "Now, gentlemen, remember this," he said. "I must tell you that because you are scientific and professional navy people, you will recognize the limitations. This ship never does actually submerge. She remains at the same depth."

As the sub approached the main show building, great curtains of bubbles were released near the viewing ports. One of the admirals said, "Well, Joe, how deep are we now?"

"I'd say periscope depth," replied Fowler.

"Gee, this is really great. How do you do it? How do you effect the water-tight security?"

So much for "truth in advertising."

Many guests were equally fooled and succumbed to the illusion. The Disneyland navy logs have recorded numerous instances of guests having "claustrophobic attacks" once the voyage got under way. The line between fantasy and reality had been blurred often in Disneyland, but never had it been as indistinguishable as on the "Voyage Through Liquid Space."

At the grand opening of the Park's most extensive and expensive additions yet, Vice President and Mrs. Richard Nixon and their two daughters

joined Walt and Lillian for the ribbon-cutting. A Disneyland employee re-membered the minor struggle that ensued. "There was just no way that the giant pair of scissors were going to cut through the ribbon. The scissors were made for ceremonial pictures, but they couldn't cut hot butter. Finally, we had to reach out and tear the ribbon in half." And with that torn ribbon on June 14, 1959, Tomorrowland moved a very large step closer to "tomorrow."

THE ONE WHO DIDN'T GET IN

Shortly after the dedication of the Submarine Voyage, the news media was handed one of its most bizarre and absurd stories ever—the non-visit of Soviet Premier Nikita Khrushchev. Khrushchev had been on a tour of the United States, and planned a visit to Disneyland while he was on the West Coast. But the American government officials simply could not be convinced that enough security precautions could be effected to safeguard his visit. The

Rumanian supergymnast Nadia Comaneci, a special visitor to Disneyland in 1984 (below), *hadn't yet been born when Nikita Khrushchev was denied a visit to Disneyland in 1959.*

The Flying Saucers landed in Tomorrowland in 1961, riding on a cushion of air (opposite). *After barely surviving five years of mechanical gremlins, the saucers vanished in 1966.*

spectacle of the head of a superpower state behaving like any kid deprived of an anticipated treat and exploding in a temper tantrum became an international incident. Park publicists must have smiled broadly to themselves at the world-wide attention.

Bob Hope quipped to an Alaskan audience, "Here we are in America's forty-ninth state, Alaska. That's halfway between Khrushchev and Disneyland."

"I don't really blame Khrushchev for jumping up and down in a rage over missing Disneyland," wrote author Herman Wouk. "There are few things more worth seeing in the United States or indeed anywhere in the world."

Walt Disney himself was greatly disappointed that Khrushchev could not visit the Park. He had a line ready for the Soviet leader's arrival: "Well, now, Mr. Khrushchev, here's my Disneyland submarine fleet. It's the eighth-largest submarine fleet in the world."

Perhaps it might have been comforting to Khrushchev had he known that his media event would blaze the way for future visits of Eastern Bloc officials. A few years later, when Soviet cosmonaut Major General Beregovoi sampled the attractions of Disneyland, he announced that he felt "twenty-five years younger." Eventually, the sight of Russian basketball teams, East German swim teams, Rumanian gymnasts (including the legendary Nadia Comaneci) became as familiar as that of burly American Rose Bowl teams and other sports squads, all lining up in front of Sleeping Beauty Castle for their "class picture" with Mickey Mouse.

THE SAUCERS HAVE LANDED

By the summer of 1961, the Submarine Voyage and the Matterhorn had become two of the most popular attractions in Disneyland. The Monorail system had been extended more than a mile to connect with the nearby Disneyland Hotel, thereby realizing its destiny as a true transportation system. Yet the ever-changing world of the future already demanded another important attraction in Tomorrowland. The "Flying Saucers," launched in August 1961, operated with the most modern space program–based technology yet developed.

Roger Broggie remembers when Walt decided to prepare a "landing pad" in Tomorrowland. "We had figured that we could move a two-thousand-pound payload if we had an air jet below with valves that allow air to come up through holes in the floor." Broggie had talked to the manufacturer who had developed the actuators that were used on the second stage of the Jupiter mis-

sile. They recommended that Disney purchase the controls, which were an overrun for the government. "We bought them and put them to use," said Broggie. "When we had the first failures, we sent them back, and they wanted to know what we had done to make them wear out like this. We estimated the actuators had cycled more than seven million times. They said that their test program had required that the actuators be cycled one million times before the government accepts them. These actuators were actually used for five seconds on the second stage of the Jupiter missile for pitch control, then their purpose was fulfilled. They said that they'd overdesigned it by seven times!"

In a press release, Joe Fowler revealed that "Disneyland had been experimenting with the Flying Saucers in Northern California for months. Because of the air-cushion principle, we have kept the tests completely under wraps."

When the Flying Saucers debuted at Disneyland, the complicated system sputtered its way to operational readiness. Giant fans located underground blew huge amounts of air up through little openings in the Saucer arena. The force of the air lifted the saucers a few inches above the floor, and held them there. Employees were "volunteered" to act as the first test pilots, and as they shifted their weight to the left or right, the saucers started careening crazily across the arena.

Over the years, the system that made the saucers fly continued to be a maintenance nightmare. Finally, in 1966, the saucers disappeared, never to be seen again.

THE "IN-BETWEENS" AT FANTASYLAND

Not everything added to Disneyland in the early days went toward increasing attraction capacity, nor even toward providing the publicity staff with major news to trumpet. In 1961, Walt was given an exquisite set of Italian marble statues of Snow White and the Seven Dwarfs, executed by European craftsmen. The figures were nestled into a quaint waterfall, wishing well, and forest environment in a secluded area next to Sleeping Beauty Castle.

It really didn't make much sense, thought many Disneyland employees. After all the major construction Walt had started during the past several years, why would he put so much effort into a Snow White wishing well? Especially when it was practically hidden, out of the mainstream of guest flow that always carried across the castle drawbridge. And especially when Disneyland wasn't even going to charge a ten-cent A coupon for it. Many began to question what they had heard about Walt Disney being a good businessman.

Walt presented a petrified tree to his wife, Lillian, as an anniversary present in 1957. She quickly donated the tree to Disneyland, where it is still on display in Frontierland.

But when the project opened, they discovered that Walt had created one of those remarkable pieces of out-of-the-way charm that doesn't shout or call attention to itself. Instead, the visitor sort of stumbles upon it, experiencing all the surprise and delight that childhood discoveries bring.

The sounds of waterfalls merge with Snow White's echolike singing of "I'm Wishing" . . . beautiful, full-grown swans sail gracefully across a moat

The Snow White Grotto and Wishing Well is one of the many special touches that complete the major scenes in Disneyland.

Looking straight down from the heights of the Swiss Family Treehouse in Adventureland can be a dizzying experience (below). The water wheel seen here actually works, carrying water to the highest room in the house, then dropping it into a bamboo plumbing system that carries the water from room to room before returning it to the river below. Adventureland's Tahitian Terrace brought the South Pacific to Southern California with fine dining and nightly entertainment (opposite, below).

that "protects" the European castle rising above the shoreline . . . a small pine forest sequesters the entire scene from the rest of Disneyland, and from the rest of the world. It is here that one begins to appreciate the subliminal genius of the Park.

In many ways, Disneyland is similar to a Disney animated film. Each of its main attractions plays the same role as the animator's "key frames" for the film, the frames that convey the extremes of the action. The "Snow White Wishing Well" functioned as one of the many "in-betweens" that linked the key frames together to complete the three-dimensional animated "film" called Disneyland.

ADVENTURELAND GOES HIGH-RISE

Many of the "in-betweens" that Disney placed in his Park related to landscaping, especially to trees of all sizes, shapes, and even ages. While driving around Colorado Springs in the late 1950s, Walt saw a sign that read "Petrified Trees for Sale." In almost no time at all, he had purchased a petrified tree for his and his wife Lillian's anniversary, and it soon found a home in Frontierland, along the banks of the Rivers of America.

In 1961, Disney asked Bill Evans to relocate a stunningly beautiful coral tree away from the Jungle River bank, so that he could replace it with what Evans called an "ersatz tree," that is, a tree made out of concrete. In order to fill the needs of the new "Tahitian Terrace" show, a much larger tree was required to house all the lights and sound systems that would be used. Evans quickly devised a revolutionary new method for transplanting the coral tree to another location in Adventureland. (Losing any kind of a tree was unthinkable to the people in the Disney organization.) After putting the tree on a "diet" by digging around the roots and washing all the soil away, he drove two large bolts through the fragile tree trunk at opposite angles. The tree was then gently lifted out of the ground and placed in its new Adventureland location, where it still thrives today.

After the artificial tree was completed at the Tahitian Terrace, Disney eyeballed the scene and discovered that they needed more height to optimize guest sightlines. "Well, it's too damned late now," muttered a construction worker to himself. Characteristically, Disney found a simple way to deal with the problem. In his inimitable fashion, he asked with great curiosity, "Why can't we just cut through the trunk and add a piece to raise it up to the height we really need?" Such a simple idea seemed totally absurd at first. It turned out to be the only solution, however, and the concrete tree was successfully "force-grown" to meet the requirements of the new show.

Between the Adventureland tree and an earlier Tom Sawyer Island tree-house, Disney had now accumulated the design experience and construction know-how to take on the first high-rise treehouse in the world: a 150-ton, man-made wonder that would rise some seventy feet over the jungle in Adventureland. Based on the 1960 Disney film hit *Swiss Family Robinson*, it would provide a spectacular view of the jungle river below from treehouse rooms fashioned from the ship's wreckage.

Disney people called the new tree *Disneyodendron semperflorens grandis*, which means "large, everblooming Disney tree." No ordinary tree, it boasted some three hundred thousand handmade vinyl leaves and thousands of bright, permanent blossoms, all wrapped around massive branches with a span of eighty feet across the jungle canopy. And they were supported by man-made banyan-like roots that burrowed deeply into the river banks below.

To add the finishing touch to this remarkable structure, each room came complete with fresh running water. A huge, "river-driven" water wheel at the tree's base provided the power for a collection device like a minibucket brigade that scooped up water and transported it to the uppermost room, where it flowed into a bamboo canal system. From there, the water would rush and twist through each treehouse section on a gravity-powered return trip to the rushing river below. It was certainly a quaint, but effective, plumbing system.

JUNGLE HUMOR

Shortly after the opening of the new Treehouse in 1962, Disney found his attention focused on an old attraction in Adventureland. He knew that the Jungle Cruise animation acted up now and then (he once quipped, "I know these alligators work. I've seen it on television"). But he found no other reason to fault his beloved jungle attraction, still one of the most popular in Disneyland. Until the day he overheard a guest's remark about it: "We don't need to go on this ride," the guest told her friends. "We've already seen it."

Surprised by the comment, Disney assigned his designers to rethink and expand several scenes. Determined to keep the Park's appeal fresh and ever-changing, he assigned Marc Davis, one of his longtime animators, to take a close look at the Jungle Cruise and develop recommendations for the new scenes.

For many years, Davis's forte had been strong, easy-to-identify visual hu-

This hippo concept sketch of 1955 (opposite, above) for the Jungle Cruise leads to its three-dimensional assembly (opposite, below), and finally to its home in the river (below), where it attacks a launch filled with jungle explorers.

mor in the Disney animated film classics. Walt Disney's ability to see the humorous side of nature in terms of human traits had already carried his True-Life Adventure films to several Academy Awards. Davis decided to add a humorous touch to Disneyland attractions in a natural extension of what Walt had already proven to be a public success. This comic touch would be applied to a number of Disneyland attractions in the future, as a "Davis signature."

In the summer of 1964, the Marc Davis fantasy-humor touch was introduced into Harper Goff's original Jungle Cruise designs, which had been inspired by the realism of the Disney True-Life Adventure films. The change from reality to fantasy was astonishing and, for some, controversial.

A rhino "makes its point" by chasing a safari party up a tree and threatening the low man on the pole with its sharp horn. Does the placement of the "Great White Hunter" at the top of the tree indicate his cowardice or his social position? Or is the whole incident just a sample of simple, innocent humor? Elephants frolic in a "sacred bathing pool," mischievously squirting water across the bow of the boat. Are those smiles on their faces or realistic expressions of playful pachyderms?

Could "true-life realism" coexist with fantasy caricatures? Could a sense of adventure be preserved in the face of cartoon-like gags? Richard Schickel,

A 1962-model pachyderm (opposite) *makes the freeway journey from the Disney Studios in Burbank to the Jungle Cruise at Disneyland. Back at WED, designer Marc Davis sketches the Trapped Safari for the makeover of the Jungle Cruise* (below).

writing in *The Disney Version*, deplored what he perceived as a "cuteness" in many of the Park's attractions that frustrated his ability to suspend disbelief. The message of Disneyland, he felt, was that "cuteness existed as an ideal in nature long before man appeared." The new Jungle Cruise sparked debates that still rage among Disneyphiles to this day. For the most part, however, the public response has been positive. Indeed, the guests seem to appreciate the departure from reality into fantasy. And the public response, as Walt liked to point out to critics, is really all that matters.

The new Jungle Cruise additions held a greater significance, however, in their promise of a new world of lifelike animation that would soon be emerging. Actually, it had begun a couple of years earlier, in 1960, when Disney elected to adapt some of his Academy Award–winning True-Life Adventure films—*Beaver Valley*, *Bear Country*, and the pioneering True-Life classic, *The Living Desert*—into a major new addition to Frontierland, "Nature's Wonderland." While it was primarily a major renovation and expansion of the existing Rainbow Caverns Mine Train attraction, the key milestone of Nature's Wonderland was buried in a press release that mentioned, for the first time anywhere, *Audio-Animatronics*. Although no one realized it at the time, it was the beginning of one of the greatest advancements in the history of Disneyland.

CHAPTER FIVE

Electronic Pixie Dust

A new door opened for us. Our whole forty-some
years here have been in the world of making things
move. Inanimate things move from a drawing board
through all kinds of little props and things.
Now we're making these dimensional human figures
move . . . animals move . . . anything move through the
use of electronics. It's all programmed . . . predetermined.
It's another dimension in the animation we have
been doing all our lives. It's a new door . . . a new
toy . . . and we hope we can really do some
exciting things in the future.

WALT DISNEY

Walt Disney saw the road to realistic animation as a quest. He had pursued it during the earliest days of the Disneyland dream, through miniature figures driven by cables and cams. But, as Roger Broggie pointed out, the limitations of technology at the time were too severe to warrant further development. Later, in 1949, Disney had written a letter to a Los Angeles patent attorney that proposed dimensional animation that could be synchronized with audio tracks of words and music. But he again ran up against the limits of technology.

A MARRIAGE MADE IN HEAVEN

When Disneyland opened in 1955, it featured three-dimensional animation in many attractions, but it was crude, unreliable, and not always convincing. Human figures could be used only in very brief scenes, such as in the Fantasyland "dark rides," where the viewers didn't have time to notice the deficiencies of the animation.

By the early 1960s, riding the surge of an expanding space program and the emerging world of electronics, the technology finally became available to realize Disney's vision. Advancements in hydraulic and pneumatic hardware helped the WED designers overcome the herky-jerky motion of earlier animation and produce fluid, lifelike movement. And new computer systems choreographed the movements precisely to the art director's commands. For Disney, the marriage of technology and entertainment was made in heaven. It was the dawning of the age of "electronic pixie dust."

CONFUCIUS SAYS

Roger Broggie remembers the first primitive attempt at creating a life-size *Audio-Animatronics* figure, long before the days of computers and electronics. "Our idea," said Broggie, "was to have a Confucius-type character in a restaurant, who could answer questions from the audience, mixed with his own sayings, all orchestrated by a live emcee."

Broggie and Wathel Rogers taxed their remarkable mechanical abilities to the limit, finding ways to stuff the head with enough controls to provide mouth movements and eye movements and blinks. At one point they installed gag false teeth that could be wound up to clack. The "brains" consisted of a solenoid, a cylindrical coil of wire that created a magnetic field to activate the controls. Finally, the head was covered with a flexible latex rubber for its skin.

Crude as it was, the Chinese head created a sensation, according to Ken Anderson. He had been invited to an office wing where the head was displayed, where he found a creature that might have come from a classic horror movie. "I couldn't see any wire," said Anderson. "Here was this head with its eyes closed, propped up on the table. A button was pushed and it came to life and started to talk to you. It was spooky . . . as spooky as anything I'd ever seen before."

Completing the horror film scenario was the maze of mechanisms that controlled the head itself. The equipment, with its mammoth size and imposing high-tech appearance, would have fit quite nicely into the lab of Dr. Frankenstein.

As intriguing as the Confucius head may have been, it was still plagued with unsolved problems, not the least of which was its fragile, easily torn rubber face. The debut of *Audio-Animatronics* would have to wait—but not for long.

Shortly after the WED designers completed their experiments with the Chinese head, they turned their efforts toward the creation of a lifelike figure of Abraham Lincoln. Since 1956, a patriotic attraction called "The Hall of Presidents" had been under development for Disneyland. Walt had envisioned it as part of a project called "Liberty Street," a re-creation of colonial America that would stand next to Main Street. Armed with the promising new *Audio-Animatronics* system (or "A.A.," as the Imagineers fondly call it), they believed that they could successfully produce the show with all the refinement and dignity that the subject called for.

Wathel Rogers remembers Walt strongly insisting that the most important thing to develop was the expression of the mouth. The staff watched TV actors with the sound turned off in order to concentrate on the movements of their mouths. Reproducing lifelike human movements was an especially difficult task, because everyone knows exactly how they are supposed to look. As they worked on this problem, they found their experience in animated films helped them make significant progress.

Then Walt returned from a vacation with an idea that was strictly for the birds.

Preceding pages: *A concept sketch for "Great Moments with Mr. Lincoln," one of the earliest* Audio-Animatronics *figures.*

This engineering concept sketch for a Tiki bird (below) *shows the details of its perch high up in the ceiling of the Enchanted Tiki Room.*

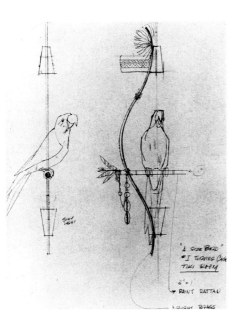

THE ENCHANTED TIKI ROOM

When Disney traveled overseas, he spent endless hours poking through flea markets and junk shops, looking for mechanical toys for his staff to take apart and study. He returned with several tiny mechanical birds whose excellent animation had impressed him. If toymakers can do this well, he thought, then our technology could make these birds absolutely sensational.

Disney put his Lincoln program on temporary hold and threw all his resources into developing life-size toucans, cockatoos, macaws, and other tropical birds. He planned to assemble the entire cast inside a Polynesian "Tiki Hut" restaurant, where they would come to life at the end of the meal and perform in concert. Soon, in his inimitable fashion, Disney had expanded the show to include Tiki drummers (idols of Polynesian mythology), singing flowers, and colorful fountains.

"For the first time in his entertainment career," the press release said, "Walt Disney is creating a restaurant. And just as his full-length animated films, True-Life Adventures, and Disneyland pioneered in their fields, Walt's creation may alter the course of many full-course meals."

America's altered state of dining, however, would not come via the Tiki restaurant. The new concept quickly outgrew its available space in the facility, until Disney had to make a choice: reduce the complexity of the production or

An artist's sketch of 1962 details the singing Tiki birds (opposite, left). *WED designers dress a flock of Tiki birds in production* (opposite, right). *The birds made their debut in 1963* (above), *instantly creating a mood of enchantment.*

eliminate the restaurant. It was an easy decision. Tiki Room, the restaurant, became Tiki Room, the attraction.

During the creation of the show, Walt often walked the Studio area, known as Pelican Alley, where many of the birds were being built and tested. (Curiously, there were no pelicans in the project.) One day, Disney arrived with famed Hollywood gossip columnist Hedda Hopper, hoping to demonstrate his new world of *Audio-Animatronics*. Stopping at one of the areas where an employee was adjusting a bird, he asked if he could make it work for his guest. The bird was powered by compressed air, but before the employee could hook it up, Walt pushed the valve on the open air line. A tremendous burst of air shot out and hit Hedda Hopper squarely in the face. The joke for weeks around the Studio was that it still didn't equal the volume of hot air she usually spread around Hollywood.

At its completion, the Tiki Room had 225 *Audio-Animatronics* performers directed by a fourteen-channel magnetic tape feeding one hundred separate speakers and controlling 438 separate actions. The show was mocked up on a Studio sound stage.

Wathel Rogers and the rest of the WED team had been programming the show by bits and pieces. Just before a visit by Walt, they put everything together on the tape for the first time. "We turned it on," said Rogers, "and it was almost as if we had programmed it backward and sideways. The flowers were singing the birds' tracks, the Tiki poles were singing the flowers' tracks, and the lights were flashing on and off sporadically. It was just a horrendous, catastrophic mess. So I was nominated to go up and tell Walt that we couldn't show it to him."

Rogers survived the debacle, and so did the "Enchanted Tiki Room." Some time later, just before a special press premiere, Disneyland employees arrived for a sneak preview. Glancing around the room, many made snap judgments about the inanimate birds that were in "freeze frame" everywhere. "So what's the big deal," they thought, playing the role of hardened show veterans. But they felt just a touch of wonder as a hostess tapped one of the cages and the bird awakened, quickly springing to life and surveying the audience below. The technology-entertainment marriage was already beginning to take control of the emotions.

Bit by marvelous bit, the entire room began to awaken. The birds, the flowers hanging in ornate boats overhead, the Polynesian carvings in the corners, the statues, the windows, and, yes, even the ceiling all came to life. A magnificent "bird mobile" descended to meet an ever-growing fountain of water emerging from the floor below. For seventeen minutes, the toughest audience that could ever be selected was totally enthralled by a stunning unveiling of the magical scenes. They laughed, sang, whistled, and applauded the arrival of a new era in Disney entertainment. But they also found that describing the new show to Disneyland guests was surprisingly and frustratingly difficult.

"What's that Tiki Room thing?" confused guests would ask. But carrying on about singing flowers and birds in an attempt to describe the show left the employees feeling somewhat akin to fools. Invariably, the guests' eyes would take on a mystified, quizzical look. Even Disney's fabled Sunday night television show, which faithfully showcased the Tiki Room from its inception, had not been able to convey its magic effectively to the public.

Finally, a new member was added to the Tiki cast: a "barker bird," which was stationed outside, just above the entrance turnstile, extolled the wonders of the show inside. The result was immediate and surprising. Guests clogged the entrance to Adventureland as they stopped to watch the gregarious bird. But they also jammed the entrance to the Tiki Room. Where humans failed to communicate, a "motor-mouthed" barker bird succeeded.

Don Jackson, a Stanford University professor of psychiatry, found himself "in awe of Disneyland" as he watched the Tiki Room show. He wrote in *Medical Opinion and Review*:

I hope the God-fearing and the God-loving folks will reserve their judgments until the very end of this article. In any case, I expect to be torn apart by the piranhas among the Beethoven Quinteters and the Bolshoisters. This is because I claim to have felt a great sense of awe, wonderment, and reverence while sitting in the synthetic, fabricated instant-Polynesian Tiki Room at Disneyland, as I have experienced in some of the great cathedrals . . . Chartres, Rheims, and Notre Dame. . . .

Coldly, simply, this wild vision was the production of the factual minds of electronic engineers. A programmed tape, or perhaps a computer, created exact mathematical sounds and movements as near to real beauty or art as faradic current applied to the vocal chords of Galli-Curci. . . .

Disney was a master executive capable of harnessing vast numbers of talented people to work out the details of his childlike vision. Like an innocent, Disney did not recognize the ordinary limitations implied by knowledge. All his creative productions realize the visions of childhood—they reach beyond the stars.

DISNEY LANDS IN THE BIG APPLE

Three thousand miles away from Disneyland, Walt's *Audio-Animatronics* quest would soon be given a dramatic boost. Robert Moses, the developer of the 1939 World's Fair in New York City, was busy planning a major encore. The New York World's Fair of 1964–65 would be held at Flushing Meadows, the same site that held his 1939 fair. Moses was determined to make his new fair one of the most lavish in history.

In search of new ideas, Moses went out to California to study the Disneyland phenomenon. He also intended to visit Walt Disney at the Studio.

When Moses arrived, Walt asked him if he would like to meet Mr. Lincoln. "Moses gave me a funny look," Walt remembered. "I said, 'Come on in and meet him!' So when we walked in the door, I said 'Mr. Lincoln, meet Mr. Moses,' and Lincoln stood up and put his hand out, and Moses went over and shook hands with him. Well, Moses is quite a showman and he said, 'I've got to have Lincoln at the fair!' But I said this is five years away anyway. But Moses wouldn't take no for an answer.

"The next thing I knew, he had gotten together with the state of Illinois and was trying to sell them on a pavilion. Before I knew it, I had my arm

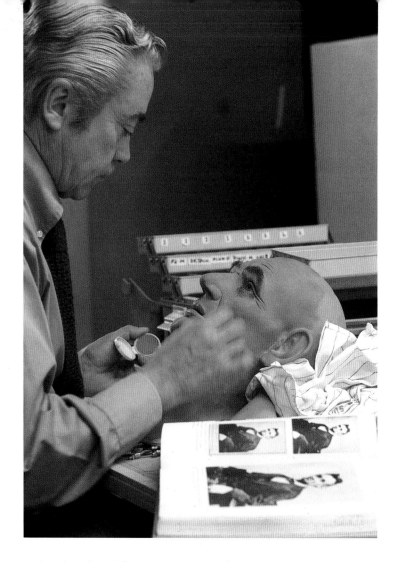

The vinyl face mask for the Abraham Lincoln Audio-Animatronics *figure gets the finishing touches.*

twisted and I said yes. We now had to get Mr. Lincoln on the road, I think, in about thirteen months."

It is curious that the next great period of Disneyland expansion should have its start here, three thousand miles away, in an area often blasé about things Disney. In addition to the Lincoln project he was producing for the state of Illinois, Walt was asked to produce three more Disneyland-type shows, for the Ford Motor Company, General Electric, and Pepsi-Cola. Walt's large-scale involvement in the fair immediately raised some eyebrows. Why his interest in putting so much effort toward a temporary exposition?

On second glance, the reason seemed evident enough. It gave Disney an opportunity to develop major shows with somebody else's money, and, at the fair's conclusion, the shows could be brought to Disneyland for a fraction of what they would have cost to create from scratch. But there was another, far more important reason, and it was kept out of sight as part of Disney's hidden agenda.

If Walt Disney had been able to go back to square one at Disneyland, with the bankers secure in the knowledge of its coming success, he would have changed one major thing dramatically. He would have found a way to acquire more land, much more land, than his original funding allowed. Walt faced a growing paradox that greatly frustrated him. It seemed that as more people fled the real world to seek refuge in Disneyland, the closer the real world crept. In order to meet the growing tourist demand for accommodations, the

Mr. Lincoln concludes his address at Disneyland. He was far better behaved there than at the New York World's Fair in 1964.

streets surrounding the Park had grown into ugly entanglements of motels with flashing neon signs competing for the tourists' attention. To Disney, it looked as if his dream had been dropped in the middle of the nightmare known as Las Vegas.

Off-limits rooms with locked doors once again became a part of the WED scene as a secret program known only as "Project X" began. It would be Disney's last and greatest dream . . . a dream for a place with enough land, according to Walt, "to hold all the ideas and plans we could possibly imagine." Project X would eventually be revealed as Walt Disney World, to be situated on a block of land in central Florida that was more than twice the size of the island of Manhattan. But first, Walt had to reassure himself that the East Coast audiences were receptive to Disneyland-style entertainment. He would never find a better opportunity to gain an honest answer than at the New York World's Fair.

THE WINKIN' BLINKIN' LINCOLN

Blaine Gibson was one of the finest sculptors ever to work for the Disney organization. But his confidence wavered when he found out that WED really had to complete the Lincoln figure. "Fortunately," he recalled, "we only had to do the one figure. The concept was reduced from 'The Hall of Presidents' to 'Great Moments with Mr. Lincoln.' But even the Lincoln show certainly

Walt and WED designer Vic Greene review the miniature model of Great Moments with Mr. Lincoln in 1963.

didn't appear to some of us the right thing to do. It seemed that we were getting into areas that were competitive with acting, something that could be done much better by live performers."

However, Gibson realized that live actors usually gave dismal performances when they tried to emulate historical figures that the public already had seen through photographs. "No matter how great the actors were," said Gibson, "they usually didn't have the physiognomy to be believable. I suspect that Walt was hoping that we could, for the first time in history, really make Lincoln look like Lincoln. Something that an actor could never do, and something that a makeup man could never do."

Gibson made Lincoln look "real" by making him larger than life. He knew that in a theater environment, the Lincoln figure would appear dwarfed, and would have to be taller than Lincoln's six-foot-four-inch frame in order to appear that size. For the visual references, Blaine called upon the work of the pioneer Civil War photographer Mathew Brady. "We probably had better access to visual information on Lincoln than on any contemporary president. Back in those early days of photography, they had to take poses that they could hold for a long time. We had enough side views, front views, and three-quarter views to do a credible job."

Gibson also worked from a life mask of Lincoln taken in 1860. No one would ever question the authenticity of his remarkable three-dimensional likeness of America's sixteenth president. But some questioned Disney's judgment. Why would he choose to feature one of the most revered Americans in his experimental show? Newspaper editorials decried Disney's audacity. They felt the idea of a "winkin' blinkin' Lincoln" was one of the most tasteless endeavors imaginable.

Wathel Rogers was painfully aware of the pitfalls. When the time for the press preview neared, he was philosophical as Lincoln's five hundred pounds of

A concept sketch depicts pterodactyls descending into the Primeval World.

hydraulic pressure smashed a chair to splinters. "It seems that, no matter, every show we open," he says, "we always have a technical problem, because we're trying systems that are experimental, ahead of their time." Rogers had a special breakaway chair readied, just in case Lincoln became destructive again.

On the night of the premiere, Disney arrived with the governors of Illinois and New York. He asked Dick Nunis if everything was ready. "No, sir," Nunis replied, "we just don't have a show. The program is still malfunctioning."

Disney did a good job of controlling his frustration. "Okay, I'll handle it," he said, as the entourage filed into the press-filled theater. "Ladies and gentlemen," he announced evenly, "there's an old saying in show business. If you're not ready, don't open the curtain. I'm sorry to say that we have a malfunction, and the show's not ready."

Disney promised them a show the following week, guaranteeing Wathel Rogers and the crew several twenty-four-hour efforts. This time, the preview showings went well. Rogers remembers how, for the first time, they even turned the tables on the ever-present Murphy's Law. "At the end of one of the first shows," Rogers said, "there was a good round of applause, as usual, when Lincoln sat down. But due to a malfunction in one of the feedback wires in his leg, he then stood back up, as if he were taking a bow. The place came apart! People cheered and clapped and generally went crazy." Take that, Mr. Murphy.

THE DINOSAURS OF FORD

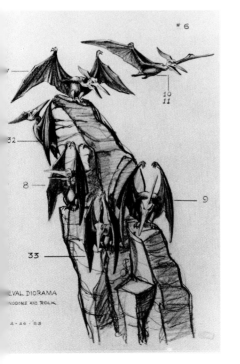

While the state of Illinois chose to sponsor a bit of history, the Ford Motor Company elected to sponsor some prehistory. Its pavilion would feature a time machine journey, in which visitors would be carried in Ford convertibles along a "Magic Skyway." On their adventure through time, they would encounter cavemen and full-size dinosaurs, brought to life through the magic of *Audio-Animatronics*. (It was the first known association of American cars and dinosaurs.) The visitors would spy on primitive man at the moment of major discoveries, such as making fire and fashioning a crude invention that later became the wheel. The grand finale carried the show into a city of the future, the realm of the Disney special-effects wizards.

The project was plagued with what had now become the usual, expected gremlins. But writer Marty Sklar faced a problem caused by human rather than technical agents. Sklar rode the Ford vehicles for seemingly endless

hours, carefully checking the narration and adjusting the timing of each scene by placing markers along the route. When he returned after some badly needed sleep, he found that a fastidious janitorial crew had scrubbed his carefully placed marks clean. For Sklar, the idea of perseverance took on renewed meaning.

Jim Macdonald was handed another kind of challenge, regarding the show's audio systems. Macdonald's wacky experiments with sound effects had provided Disney with the largest audio library of its type in the world. Macdonald had also supplied the voices for many Disney cartoon characters, from yodeling dwarfs in *Snow White* to Mickey Mouse himself. (Disney had originally supplied the voice of Mickey, but no longer had the time.)

Giving voice to dinosaurs and cavemen almost left Macdonald speechless . . . literally. The primitive grunts of prehistoric man were easy, but the ferocious snarls and thunderous roars of fighting dinosaurs had put such a strain on his vocal chords that they loosened, like slack strings on a guitar, and went temporarily silent. But not before he accomplished his mission. Passengers aboard the Magic Skyway were astonished by sounds they had certainly never heard before.

WALT IN PROGRESSLAND

A few years before the fair, the General Electric lamp division had visited WED and wanted to sponsor an attraction in Disneyland. John Hench re-

members working on a show called "Edison Square," the story of progress through electricity. It captured much of the feeling of a popular play of the time, Thornton Wilder's *Our Town.*

The idea resurfaced with the impending arrival of the New York fair. General Electric decided to go with the concept, changing the name to "Progressland," a title consistent with its current marketing motto, "Progress is our most important product."

The Progressland Pavilion was designed as a giant carrousel in which the audience would rotate around a central core of scenes, visiting a family as its life-style changed from 1890 through 1920 to 1940 and up to the present. The father of the family would present nostalgic ideas about the home and about the progress General Electric had brought to each era. Even so, they were always looking forward to "A Great Big Beautiful Tomorrow," as the show's theme song consistently pointed out.

As usual, Disney kept closely involved in the show's design. When his staff worked on a comical 1920s scene in which lazy, beer-drinking "Cousin Orville" was to sit in a bathtub with his back to the audience, Walt questioned the staging. He turned the tub around to face the audience, took off his shoes and socks, and jumped in. "He'd wiggle his toes, don't you think?" was Disney's conclusion. It was another of the subliminal touches that had become a Disney trademark.

Of course, the family's home appliances, all by General Electric, were often spotlighted, later prompting WED chief Dick Irvine to call it, in retro-

Walt Disney, Gerald Philippe, president of General Electric, and Steven Van Voorhis review the Carousel of Progress building for the New York World's Fair. The building was later restyled to fit into Tomorrowland for its Disneyland opening in 1967.

spect, "a refrigerator show." Irvine knew full well, though, the importance of "refrigerator shows," the kind of presentations that met the needs of the sponsor-client, the audience, and the Disney organization. The participation of major corporations would help bring the increasingly complex and sophisticated Disney concepts to reality. It was both a philosophical and practical marriage of American industry and Disney showmanship.

A concept sketch details Cousin Orville's "air-cooled" bathtub in the Carousel of Progress. Walt Disney later helped art direct the final scene.

THE HAPPIEST CRUISE THAT EVER SAILED

Perhaps the most astonishing Disney accomplishment of the New York World's Fair was "It's a Small World." Pepsi-Cola, which had a tie-in with UNICEF, wanted a children's attraction for the fair. For the first time in his remarkable career, Admiral Joe "Can-Do" Fowler said, "Can't do." With the fair less than a year away, Fowler didn't see how the pavilion could possibly be designed and built in time for the grand opening. Pepsi reluctantly went to look elsewhere.

When Disney heard about Fowler's conversation, he became furious. "He was mad as hell at Joe," recalled Dick Irvine. "He said, 'I'll make those decisions. Tell Pepsi I'll do it!'"

Walt had long talked about doing an attraction featuring animated dolls representing the children of the world, all singing in harmony and peace. He quickly called a series of story sessions to develop this concept.

For designer Rolly Crump, the "impossible" one-year deadline presented

Concept sketch for the Arabian Nights in It's a Small World (left). At WED, the finishing touches are applied to a pair of dolls prior to their installation in It's a Small World (right). Walt and designer Rolly Crump review the Tower of the Four Winds, the kinetic marquee for It's a Small World at the 1964–65 New York World's Fair (opposite).

a golden opportunity. He had begun his career in animation by "seeing spots": the spots on the dogs in the animated film classic *101 Dalmatians*. The animators sketched out the dogs and their actions, but left the tedious task of drawing all the little spots on the dalmatians to a special crew. "I almost lost my mind trying to keep the spots coordinated on the dogs," Crump remembers with a shudder. With the Small World project, he graduated to working closely with Walt, along with Marc Davis, Claude Coats, and talented color stylist Mary Blair, whose childlike designs could be seen throughout the pavilion. Crump designed the dynamic visual marquee called "The Tower of the Four Winds," a 120-foot-tall mobile that would swing and sway in the winds that blew across Flushing Meadows.

Small World used an innovative ride system which would, of course, find its way back to Disneyland. The visitors boarded small, flat-bottomed boats and cruised through the show building along a winding canal of water. In contrast to the noisy, low-capacity dark-ride cars at Disneyland, the Small World boats were quiet, reliable, and, because each could carry nearly two dozen people, provided an extremely high hourly guest capacity. The WED engineers called it "a real people-eater," a term that was kept out of the press releases for obvious reasons.

Working in high gear, the WED crew mocked up the entire ride in full-scale on a sound stage at the Studio. They placed and tested the *Audio-Animatronics* children as soon as they came off the mechanical assembly line. The sound-stage area looked like a Hollywood version of Santa's workshop, as more

Marc Davis, Walt, and Mary Blair check the design for It's a Small World. Mary was responsible for the marvelous color-styling of the attraction.

than 250 animated toys were carefully handcrafted. The publicity release even kept track of the materials used: "195 pounds of glitter, 57 gross of jewels, 370 yards of braid, 28 dozen tassels, feathers and ostrich fluff. For children's 'hair' and animal 'fur,' they glued on marabou, ostrich plumes, goose feathers and pheasant tails, using five gallons of glue a week."

Frantic as the workshops were, they could not match the confusion of the first concepts for the show's sound tracks. "Each of the dolls was to sing its national anthem," said Disney. "The whole thing turned out to be pretty rotten. Everybody singing a different tune was simply a bad idea." Disney kept looking for a good idea. He turned to his talented songwriting team, brothers Richard and Robert Sherman, who had contributed many memorable songs for Disneyland, including the theme for the Enchanted Tiki Room. They would later win two Oscars for their work on *Mary Poppins*, but were currently hard at work on the theme song for the "Progressland" show.

"We walked into WED and saw a mock-up of the model, with all those wonderful doll figures," said Dick Sherman, the excitable melody-writing half of the team. "It was a marvelous sight to see," he continued. "But it was silent. Walt told us about the national-anthem disaster. He wanted something really simple and easy to catch on. There was a big problem here and it really had to do with the children in the show. Everybody knows that kids grow into adults, and it's adults that keep getting the world messed up. But in the small world of children, everybody loves each other. Then we thought of a concept. Why can't we all just be together, we only have one world to live on?"

The concept grew into what would become perhaps the most memorable and popular song in Disney history. Even today, more than two decades later, schoolchildren can often be heard singing Sherman's hopeful lyrics.

> There's so much that we share,
> That it's time we're aware,
> It's a small world after all.

DISNEY—GIANT AT THE FAIR

"What other person in the world," one writer asked, "would have been so venturesome, so rash, so seemingly foolhardy as to contract with Pepsi-Cola, Ford, General Electric and the State of Illinois to present four extravagantly expensive attractions, all of which were in the experimental stage, with deadlines that none of the military services or the companies themselves would have considered possible to meet?

"Yet not one of his men at WED felt put upon, and the reason is clear. If you are one of a picked group, and have been given the chance to pursue the occupation you like best, you are willing to make an extra effort."

It took that extra effort on the part of everyone at Disney. The WED staff, Studio employees, and the operating personnel quickly established performance standards that had never been seen in a world exposition before. When the fair was over, four of the five most popular shows were Disney's. And the press reaction matched the public's enthusiasm, perhaps best exemplified by a headline in *Look* Magazine: "Walt Disney—Giant at the Fair."

It gave the exhausted WED designers a tremendous boost in morale, and the major sponsors a tremendous boost in confidence in "Walt Disney presents . . ." For Disney himself, it was a personal triumph. Now he knew that Project X—Project Walt Disney World—could be a reality. But first he headed back to California. Included with Walt's luggage were his four World's Fair shows, all addressed to Disneyland.

HOMECOMING

"The past ten years have just sort of been a dress rehearsal. We're just getting started, so if any of you starts to rest on your laurels, just forget it!"

When It's a Small World came to Disneyland in 1965, the Tower of the Four Winds had been left behind in New York. Disneyland guests cruised by unique topiary gardens and a kinetic international facade that would soon become one of the most-remembered Disneyland sights (below). Walt and a hostess greet Louis Lundborg, the chairman of the Bank of America, just before the opening of It's a Small World in 1965, which the Bank of America sponsored in Disneyland (opposite).

It was the summer of 1965. Walt Disney was addressing his staff during the "Tencennial Celebration" of Disneyland when he threw them this challenge. Actually, after the fair, if anyone should have pulled back to rest on his laurels, it was Disney. Instead, he actually seemed to increase his intensity. On one front, Disney kept the fire burning brightly on the Florida project. On the other, Disneyland quickly began to reap the benefits of the fair.

Mr. Lincoln was the first to arrive. He was actually a clone of the New York edition, having been built and programmed while the fair was still open. This enabled Walt to premiere "Great Moments with Mr. Lincoln" in the Main Street Opera House exactly ten years after Disneyland first opened its gates on July 17, 1955. The arrival of the first World's Fair show was a portent of things to come.

It's a Small World moved into Fantasyland the following year, in June 1966. The Tower of the Four Winds mobile had been left behind at the fairgrounds. In its place, Rolly Crump blended whimsical versions of famed international architecture into a spectacular, kinetic facade. A huge animated clock tower launched a colorful parade of toys as it chimed out the arrival of each new hour.

Louis Lundborg, longtime business associate and head of Bank of America, accompanied Walt at the opening ceremonies. He, too, had shown his faith in Disney, by having his company take over sponsorship of the show when it moved to Disneyland. The opening day press release provided a description of the activities.

"With the help of gaily costumed children from many nations, Walt Disney dedicated Disneyland's newest attraction Monday, by mingling the waters of the oceans and seas around the world with Small World's Seven Seaways." The mixing of the water was no publicity hoax. Disney files, for exam-

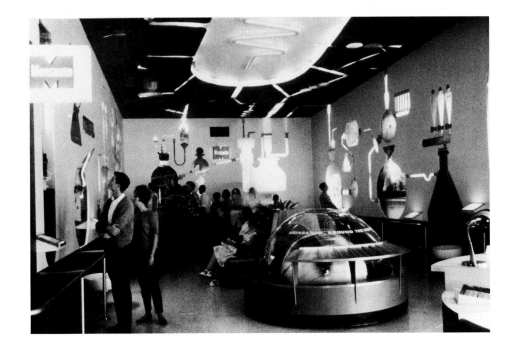

Walt, designers, and corporate sponsors review the scale model for the new Tomorrowland in 1966 (opposite, above). Walt Disney during one of his last walk-throughs with his key WED designers in 1966 planning the new Tomorrowland (opposite, below). Guests take a last look at the Hall of Chemistry (right) before it gives way to Adventure Through Inner Space.

ple, still show a billing that was paid for the sum of $21.86 for water received from a Caribbean source.

The press release continued, "Ten thousand balloons, peace doves, fireworks, and a parade of more than 500 youngsters in native costumes gave 'Bon Voyage' to the new adventure. The ceremonies were attended by 1,500 consular officials, press guests, and other dignitaries."

A few days later, the dinosaurs from New York took up residence at Disneyland, in the "Primeval World." The new attraction formed a spectacular climax to the now-familiar Grand Canyon Diorama along the Disneyland Railroad. After the guests on the trains viewed the Grand Canyon, they were treated to a look at a prehistoric canyon filled with roaring dinosaurs, screeching pterodactyls, and flowing lava. The Grand Canyon's inanimate inhabitants soon paled in contrast to the "live" prehistoric critters that lived next door.

The success of Progressland at the fair led the General Electric Corporation to Disneyland. This time Progressland would be called "The Carousel of Progress." More important, though, it had a sort of positive "domino effect" on all of Tomorrowland. The impending presence of General Electric and its renowned show in Disneyland gave Walt new leverage to talk to other major corporations.

McDonnell-Douglas agreed to a new, more exciting "Flight to the Moon." Meanwhile, the chemical giant Monsanto decided it had to forsake its now-lackluster "Hall of Chemistry" for an intriguing "Adventure Through Inner Space." And Goodyear joined up, sponsoring the "PeopleMover," a newly developed WED transportation system that would whisk guests around the new land of the future.

Disneyland had not seen a busier time since its initial construction. In the midst of all the exciting activities, it was remarkable that Walt was able to keep his secret. Only a handful of people knew about his illness.

CHAPTER SIX

After Disney

*I think by this time my staff, my young group of
executives, and everyone else are convinced that Walt is right.
The quality will out. And so I think they're going to stay
with that policy because it's proved that it's a good business policy.
Give the people everything you can give them. Keep the place as clean
as you can keep it. Keep it friendly, you know. Make it a real
fun place to be. I think they're convinced and I think they'll
hang on . . . if . . . as you say . . . well, after Disney.*

WALT DISNEY

"After Disney" began on December 15, 1966. An acute circulatory collapse resulting from lung cancer robbed Walt of the chance to see the realization of Walt Disney World, or the completion of the many Disneyland attractions still on the drawing boards.

"WE'LL NEVER SEE HIS LIKE AGAIN"

It is often said that the significance of an event can be measured by how well people remember what they were doing at the time of the occurrence. For those who were there, who doesn't remember what they were doing when they heard the news of Pearl Harbor, or the assassination of John Kennedy? Those who worked for him and those who were captivated by his magical worlds will always remember the passing of Walter Elias Disney.

The news hit Disneyland like a thunderbolt. There was great confusion as flags went to half-mast, then to full mast, and back to half again. One side wanted to recognize Walt's death by closing. Others cited show business tradition: "He would have wanted the show to go on." Tradition prevailed, and Disneyland sadly carried on.

One teacher reported that his students wept uncontrollably when they heard the news. They had lost a surrogate father, grandfather, and close friend all at the same time. Disney employees had lost all of the above, along with a boss. The remarks of Eric Sevareid on television that evening spoke for everyone:

It would take more time than anybody has around the daily news shops to think of the right thing to say about Disney.

He was an original, not just an American original, but an original, period. He was a happy accident, one of the happiest this century has experienced. And judging by the way it's been behaving, in spite of all Disney tried to tell it about laughter, love, children, puppies, and sunrises, the century hardly deserved him.

He probably did more to heal or at least soothe troubled human spirits than all the psychiatrists in the world. There can't be many adults in the allegedly civilized parts of the globe who did not inhabit Disney's mind and imagination at least for a few hours and feel better for the visitation.

It may be true, as somebody said, that while there is no highbrow in a lowbrow, there is some lowbrow in every highbrow.

Preceding pages: *The Sword in the Stone in Fantasyland awaits a new challenger.*

But what Disney seemed to know was that while there is very little grown-up in every child, there is a lot of child in every grown-up. To a child, this weary world is brand-new, gift-wrapped. Disney tried to keep it that way for adults.

By the conventional wisdom, mighty mice, flying elephants, Snow White and Happy, Grumpy, Sneezy and Dopey—all these were fantasy, escapism from reality. It's a question of whether they are any less real, any more fantastic than intercontinental missiles, poisoned air, defoliated forests, and scrap iron on the moon. This is the age of fantasy, however you look at it, but Disney's fantasy wasn't lethal. People are saying we'll never see his like again.

REFLECTIONS

For Marty Sklar, Disney's passing had a special touch of sadness to it. He remembered a conversation in which Walt remarked, "I'm not Walt Disney anymore. Walt Disney is a thing. It's grown to become a whole different meaning than just one man."

Edith Efron had made a similar observation in *TV Guide*: "He is one of the few men in show business whose name stands for something significantly larger than their work. To say Walt Disney is to pay subtle compliment to the human race."

Shortly after the conversation with Walt Disney, Sklar attempted to define the somewhat esoteric "new meaning" of the Disney name in an emotional film that would push all the right buttons in any Disneyphile.

"We called it *The Disney Image*," remembers Sklar. "At the end of the first screening for Walt there was absolute silence for what seemed like an eternity. Then he slowly got up and made just one comment as he left. 'I feel like I've just seen my own eulogy.'" An ironic comment that, unfortunately, had been only a touch ahead of its time.

In an interview shortly after Walt's death, Ward Kimball, one of the Disney Studio's "nine old men" (a term used to refer to Walt's key animators from the Studio's golden age), talked of his boss being driven by intense purpose.

"I really feel that Walt, after a certain time, had a date with destiny," said Kimball. "Even though he was building something that was fun to him, he never lost sight of the fact that it was all Walt Disney. It was a worldwide name. After the Park, and after the TV show, he was assured a niche in history. He wanted Disneyland to become an official post office, which the United States government wouldn't do. He wanted the freeways to put Disneyland on

one of their big green signs, which they wouldn't do, and he couldn't understand why. He felt Disneyland *was* a city, and maybe he was right. It has a population of more than fifty thousand on many days.

"Even though Walt played the role of the bashful tycoon who was embarrassed in public, he knew exactly what he was doing at all times."

America's businessmen agreed. In a poll designed to select the country's ten greatest deceased businessmen, Disney trailed only Henry Ford, finishing ahead of such legends as Andrew Carnegie, Thomas Edison, John D. Rockefeller, and Alexander Graham Bell. One businessman commented, "Disney has proved that high dedication to social and moral values, and being a good businessman, need not conflict."

Like many employees, Kimball was less certain about the future. "I think that any organization that was built by one man, one man's tastes and choices, will have a little tough time adjusting to the rule of the committee, where decisions are split among a group of people," said Kimball. "That's the one advantage of having one man. Good or bad, he makes a decision and you run with it."

By now, however, the Disney organization had so much momentum that key executives Roy Disney, Donn Tatum, and Card Walker got through the adjustment period fairly smoothly. It was a tribute to Roy's leadership that he didn't pull back the reins financially on the creative organization as it started to get back on its feet.

ATTACK IN THE CARIBBEAN

The first new land at Disneyland since its opening in 1955 was also the last major project that Walt supervised. "Disneyland has always had a big river and a Mississippi stern-wheeler," he said shortly before his death. "It seemed appropriate to create a new attraction at the bend of the river. And so, New Orleans Square came into being—a New Orleans of a century ago when she was the 'Gay Paree' of the American frontier."

There would be elegant restaurants, flower marts, Creole cafés, and quaint shops. The big attraction, though would be "Pirates of the Caribbean." Today, more than twenty years after its debut, it is still considered by many to be the greatest adventure in Disneyland. And one of the great tragedies of Disney's passing was that he never saw Pirates open to the public.

"The Pirates were on the drawing boards for years," remembered Dick Irvine. "Back in the late fifties, it was going to be a wax museum. Then we were going to make it a walk-through. We even started construction, but when the New York fair came along, we just left Disneyland alone for two years."

When they returned from the fair, they brought back a great deal of knowledge about moving large masses of people. Dick Nunis, ever the operations efficiency expert, hammered away at Disney time and time again to make Pirates a ride-through attraction instead of the walk-through experience the WED designers were planning. Walt finally agreed to use the same boat system that had been so successful on It's a Small World. But that was to be the only similarity to "the happiest cruise that ever sailed."

Indeed, Walt's idea of the cruise through Pirates of the Caribbean would take guests past scenes of drunken pirates pillaging a seacoast village and ultimately burning it to the ground. When Marc Davis started to work on the project, he considered the attraction more like a horror film. "I thought, none of this is Disney," he said. "But when I started reading everything I could find

Marc Davis creates concept sketches for Pirates of the Caribbean in 1965 (left). The walls of his office would soon be plastered with hundreds of sketches, such as this sketch (1964) of a drunken pirate (above and opposite, above) showing extremes of animation in the scene.

on pirates, I found that damn few of them were ever killed in sea battles like we'd always heard. Most of them lost their lives by venereal disease picked up in brothels."

Davis was probably the best choice to help turn the X-rated story material into family fun at Disneyland. If he could design "happy elephants" and "cute, cuddly dinosaurs," then he could certainly handle G-rated pirates. The prolific Davis soon filled his office walls with sketches of swashbuckling, drunken, yet amazingly lovable fun-seeking pirates.

Meanwhile, Claude Coats began to work his usual magic with lighting and colors to create dramatic, exciting backgrounds for Davis's pirate characters. "I have always believed the story is the thing that is really first, and the animation is the thing that tells the story," said Coats. "The background has to support all that, it has to add the proper mood and give the characters the proper space and lighting to work in. But the backgrounds had to be balanced carefully. You can't make them overdone to the point of being distracting."

Several of Coats's scenes indeed proved to be distracting. After Illusioneer Yale Gracey saw Claude's concept for a burning city, he went about designing a brand-new fire effect. When the Disneyland fire marshal saw how real Yale's fire looked in the burning city, he requested that the effect be programmed to shut down if a real fire alarm were set off. Otherwise, he didn't think the firemen would be able to find out where the real fire was. Score one for WED Special Effects.

An intricate miniature model of Pirates of the Caribbean is assembled in 1966.

Pirates of the Caribbean, one of the most popular Disneyland attractions, took years to develop. In the original (1966) scale study model of the attraction, corsairs ransack the burning town (opposite, above, left). Guests glide past as the town mayor gets a dunking at the hands of the pirates while the members of the city council await their turn (opposite, above, right), and watch the special pirate auction action (opposite, below). These pirate figures under construction at MAPO seem to be very comfortable (above). MAPO (from Mary Poppins, *the profitable Disney film in release at the time MAPO was formed) is a manufacturing and production arm of WED.*

Sculptor Blaine Gibson was called upon to transform Davis's drawings into figures. This meant translating a two-dimensional concept into a three-dimensional reality, in addition to satisfying the technical requirements of the *Audio-Animatronics* mouths and eyes. Gibson's background in animation had given him a special talent. For animated films, he had had to learn how to communicate visually in the shortest possible time. In the few seconds his scenes lasted, they had to communicate something about the character on the screen. Gibson carried this experience over into three-dimensional sculpting for *Audio-Animatronics* characters.

"In a ride system," Gibson says, "you only have a few seconds to say something about a figure through your art. So we exaggerate their features, especially the facial features, so they can be quickly and easily understood from a distance. If you examined them closely, you'd find the nose, the cheekbones, the ears, the eyes all somewhat exaggerated. The frowns and the grins are all exaggerated, too, because we have to instantly communicate 'good guy' or 'bad guy.' We try to provide the illusion of life."

The Pirates of the Caribbean in 1966, plus one.

For Pirates of the Caribbean, Gibson had to communicate fear, drunkenness, joy, shyness, aggressiveness, and, most of all, happiness, in a cast of 119—64 humans and 55 animals. Meanwhile, the American optical business got the largest and strangest order in its history . . . for dozens of artificial eyes, all tinged with hangover bloodshot red.

While Gibson and Davis figured out what the pirates looked like, Xavier Atencio figured out what they would say. Or, for the most part, sing. "When we did 'Yo Ho, a Pirate's Life for Me,'" said Atencio, "we couldn't have a beginning or an end, because you didn't know where you were going to come into the song in the ride. Each verse had to make some kind of sense, no matter when you heard it."

For Atencio, the spoken script was equally challenging. "To set the mood for a show like this," he said, "you had to sort of become a pirate yourself. I think my Spanish background helped me to write the exchanges between the pirate captain and the defenders of the fort."

Atencio was dismayed when he heard his script played back in a full mock-up at WED. As he and Disney walked through the scenes, he couldn't

At MAPO in 1966, a clay sculpture of a pirate figure is covered in a thin layer of rubber to create a mold (left). The rubber is later peeled off the clay and the inside surface of the rubber covered in fiberglass. When the fiberglass hardens, the rubber is peeled off once again, revealing a duplicate of the clay sculpture. Sculptor George Snowden works on a full-size drunken pirate (right), based on the miniature figure at right.

understand a word that was being said. Apologetically, he turned to Walt and said, "Gee, I guess it's pretty hard to understand them."

Disney replied, "Don't worry about it. It's like a cocktail party. People come to cocktail parties, and they tune in a conversation over here, then a conversation over there. Each time the guest comes through here, they'll hear something else. That'll bring them back time and again!"

In the spring of 1967, just a few months after Walt died, his greatest attraction opened in the new land of New Orleans Square. Today, some two decades later, his words are still ringing true. Pirates of the Caribbean continues to "bring them back time and again."

A WORLD ON THE MOVE

Following closely on the heels of the Pirates, the new Tomorrowland debuted in the summer of 1967. It signaled a great leap forward. This was the first time in years that the "land of the future" could shed its Walt Disney–bestowed nickname, "Todayland."

This concept sketch of 1966 shows the entrance to the new Tomorrowland that Walt Disney never saw completed (below).

In one of the new attractions, Adventure Through Inner Space (1966), guests would be "miniaturized" to explore the nucleus of an atom (below).

The entrance to the new Tomorrowland in 1967.

The Carousel of Progress led the way. Its arrival at Disneyland, fresh from the New York World's Fair, had been the impetus for redesigning the entire land. Adventure Through Inner Space, the first brand-new attraction, transported guests through a giant microscope and "miniaturized" them to the size of an atom. The show, which relied on special effects rather than on *Audio-Animatronics* figures, was blessed with a remarkable new ride system, which WED called the "Omnimover." The ride vehicles, called "Atomo-biles," were two-passenger, oval-shaped pods that surrounded the guests and allowed them to see only forward. The Atomobiles could, however, turn left and right or even travel backward. For the first time, the designers could "edit" the scenes on a ride, using the eyes of the guests as a motion-picture camera. By turning the vehicles left or right, the designers could aim the guests directly at a specific scene, then "cut" the scene by spinning the car in the opposite direction. It was the ultimate marriage between motion-picture storytelling and three-dimensional entertainment.

The Atomobiles carried the guests on a journey through environments that dramatically increased in scale as the ride progressed. It had the effect of a sort of scientific *Alice in Wonderland*, as guests would "shrink" en route to the tiny nucleus of an atom. Claude Coats had redefined the meaning of "forced perspective."

After the show opened, it seemed that Xavier Atencio would have to re-define the meaning of human behavior. "We did Adventure Through Inner Space with a big plate-glass effect," Atencio said. "The kids would go in there and spit on the glass. We had also designed the sets to be close to the cars. It gave more of a show to have these effects surrounding you up close. But the kids reached out and literally tore the sets to pieces. Anything they could touch, they grabbed. I guess when they were isolated in groups of two, they were more prone to misbehavior."

To prevent future problems with misbehaving guests, the WED design-ers developed a new concept, and gave it a new term in Disney jargon. All future attractions would keep props and set pieces out of reach of even seven-foot "kids." It was euphemistically dubbed "the envelope of protection"— protection for the sets this time, not for the guests.

Directly across from Inner Space, the popular Circarama gave way to a much-improved new *"Circle-Vision"* system, whose larger, 35-millimeter film not only provided a sharper picture but reduced the number of projectors from eleven to nine. *America the Beautiful* was the first film to premiere in the new format. The system became a cornerstone for Disney exposition film produc-

Mission Control in the Flight to the Moon attraction featured the first combination of Audio-Animatronics *figures and a live actor.*

tions that would later travel to Canada, China, and many other countries around the world.

Travel "out of this world," however, was handled through the new "Flight to the Moon" attraction. Here, a new wrinkle was added that was both effective and at the same time downright eerie. Before ascending to the moon, guests went through "Mission Control" to meet a cast of *Audio-Animatronics* technicians. The live host or hostess would actually engage the programmed mission control chief in conversation. It was all quite believable, as long as the live figure asked the right questions—the Chief, "Mr. Morrow," was not about to change his tape-recorded dialogue.

Soon after man actually landed on the moon, the WED designers went NASA one better by launching guests on a "Mission to Mars." Though the show was brand-new, it retained the very popular Mr. Morrow as mission control chief.

New, high-altitude "Rocket Jets" replaced the long-popular "Astro Jets." They twirled madly about, some ninety feet above the Tomorrowland promenade. And the extraordinary PeopleMover moved in to link together all

The Circle-Vision *camera captures the Grand Canyon in all its 360-degree splendor for the film "American Journeys"* (below), *which debuted in Tomorrowland in 1984. The Rocket Jets spin high above Tomorrowland* (opposite).

the elements of Tomorrowland. The opening day press release described it as "a series of vehicles that never stop moving . . . even when passengers are boarding or debarking . . . silent trains that glide along at predetermined, varying speeds . . . automatically spaced vehicles that can't collide . . . motor-less cars that eliminate the chance of one vehicle stalling all the others . . . compartment doors that slide open and close by themselves . . . a transportation system on which passengers never have to wait for the journey to begin."

On any crowded day, however, guests almost always had a wait, because the escalators that led to the PeopleMover (called "Speedramps") were either malfunctioning or shut down. If one person slowed down or stopped at the

This series of illustrations (opposite) *demonstrates one of the startling transformations that greet guests about to explore the rooms of the Haunted Mansion.*

top, the rest of the people following would jam up behind like falling dominoes.

Despite such annoyances, the PeopleMover joined the twirling Rocket Jets, rotating Carousel of Progress, soaring Skyway buckets, the Autopia cars, the Submarines, and hordes of strolling guests to provide an astonishingly kinetic Tomorrowland that lived up to its billing as "A World on the Move."

GHOSTBUSTERS '69

It shouldn't have been too surprising that the first post–Walt Disney attraction would be burdened with controversy.

As far back as 1965, Disneyland had been promoting an upcoming addition called "The Haunted Mansion." "The world's greatest collection of 'actively retired ghosts will soon call this Haunted Mansion 'home,'" said the press release. "Walt Disney and his 'Imagineers' are now creating 1,001 eerie illusions. Marble busts will talk. Portraits that appear normal one minute will change before your eyes. And, of course, ordinary ghost tricks (walking through solid walls, disappearing at the drop of a sheet) will also be seen . . . and felt."

The Haunted Mansion building had been completed for years, remaining unoccupied along the banks of the Rivers of America. Walt's obligations for the 1964 New York World's Fair had forced him to put the Mansion's design on hold, and, in the years following the fair, too many other projects took priority. But in 1968, its time had come.

Like Pirates, the Haunted Mansion was at first scheduled to be a walk-through attraction. But the ever-pressing need for more high-capacity "people-eater" shows led to an adaptation of the Omnimover system that had been used for the Inner Space attraction. For this show, the Omnimover cars were dubbed "Doom Buggies." And this time, the Imagineers remembered the "envelope of protection."

It was difficult to find anybody at WED who did not, at one time or another, work on the project. "There were too many people," said Marc Davis. "I think we had a lot of confusion because Walt had not been gone all that long. I think there were a lot of great ideas, but when you have too many people of equal clout, nobody's about to say, 'Hey, wait a minute! Let's do it this way,' which Walt would have done in a moment."

The situation recalled Ward Kimball's fears about committee rule. In one corner were those who felt that, ghosts being scary to begin with, the

Overleaf: *Guests riding the "Doom Buggies" (below, right)* through the inner sanctums of the Haunted Mansion may find themselves giving a ride to some dubious hitchhikers (left). *The early, "frightful" concept of a decrepit mansion drawn in 1966 (above, right)* lost out to the well-manicured mansion we know today.

show needed to be lightened up. "Look at all the little kids who are frightened by the witch in the Snow White ride," they argued.

In the other corner, equally vocal designers insisted that guests would expect a big chill in anything called a Haunted Mansion. "People love to be scared," they replied.

Would Disney himself have opted for more "fright" or "light"? "When we were doing the building," recalled Claude Coats, "Walt wanted it looking fresh and new, while nearly everyone else thought it should look old and dilapidated. Everyone expects a residence for ghosts to be run-down. But Walt was always looking for the unexpected." "We'll take care of the outside," he used to say. "The ghosts can take care of the inside."

The debate took place in the mid-1960s, an era in American entertainment when *The Sound of Music* and other great, uplifting musicals reigned at the box office. Such scare films as *Poltergeist, Raiders of the Lost Ark,* and *Alien* were still light-years away from the scene.

Eventually, the designers on the "light" side won out, and the immaculate, friendly-looking Southern mansion became a "happy haunting ground." A call went out for a merry, upbeat song in the same "spirit" as "A Pirate's Life for Me." Once again, Marc Davis launched a barrage of sketches, this time depicting "grim grinning ghosts." In his own way, he became a ghostbuster.

After all those years of empty promises, it was little wonder that the newly inhabited Haunted Mansion generated tremendous interest on its grand opening. It was the most anticipated premiere in the history of Disneyland,

and quickly led the Park to new records in attendance levels. A few "ghosts of arguments past," however, still lingered in the shadows of the exit area. Here and there, one occasionally heard a guest comment, "I thought this was going to be scarier." But it wasn't heard from the little kids.

THE INVASION OF DISNEYLAND

The following summer brought an "attraction" to Disneyland that nobody wanted. The student activist movement that had begun in Berkeley in 1964 and, fed by the discontent with the Vietnam War, had swept across the nation, reached its peak in that year, 1970. No institution more idealistically represented America than Disneyland, and so radical student papers declared the Park a target to be invaded. The invasion would be held on the twenty-fifth anniversary of the Hiroshima bombing, to symbolize the American bombing raids then being carried out in Southeast Asia.

When it became clear that student activists were starting to gather in the Orange County area, Disneyland officials fretted about whether or not to close the Park. Roy Disney suggested to Dick Nunis that the Park be shut down for the day. "What about tomorrow, or the next day, or the next?" countered Nunis. "What about the people who've planned their vacations around us? Sooner or later, we're going to have to face up to this!"

Nunis prevailed, and Disneyland stayed open. About seventy-five long-haired youths were turned away at the gate for a number of violations of Park standards for admittance, including intoxication, possession of marijuana, lack of shoes and shirts. Some three hundred others were allowed to purchase tickets and enter the Park.

Disneyland employees, supervision, and security, backed up by out-of-sight riot police from Orange County, implored the youths to enjoy themselves while respecting the other guests in the Park. It was to no avail, however. It soon became clear that their mission was to create another "media event," which usually ended in full-scale rioting.

Students invaded and took over Tom Sawyer Island, where they replaced the American flag with the flag of the Viet Cong. News cameras clicked and movie film rolled. Snake-dancing around the Plaza, they began to shout obscenities at everyone in sight. Finally, the moment of confrontation became inevitable. The hidden riot teams emerged in a show of force and evicted the youths—a move that probably also protected them from the rising anger of some thirty thousand guests who had had their day ruined. The Park closed

five hours early, after offering visitors either free admission the next day or a cash refund. Disneyland survived "Yippie Day" relatively unscathed. And the national outpouring of outraged sentiment ironically seemed to prove for a moment an old saying: "The only bad publicity is *no* publicity."

THE FLORIDA HILLBILLIES

In a sense, Pirates and the Haunted Mansion were the first ride-through musical shows; as viewers rode by, they caught brief performances from the cast. "Country Bear Jamboree" went several steps further, to create a theater musical, which posed its own unique set of challenges, miles removed from the original *Audio-Animatronics* figure. Lincoln delivering a dignified speech was one thing, but a kinetic musical stage performer would severely test the dynamics of the *Audio-Animatronics* system.

The test came in 1971, and, just like Lincoln, it first occurred on the East Coast. This time, though, it would be in Florida instead of New York. The Country Bear Jamboree became one of the smash hits at the newly opened Walt Disney World resort. To the tune of foot-stomping country music, the Country Bears led a corny but lovable revue featuring such acts as the Five Bear Rugs, Big Al, and the Mae West of the bear set, Teddi Bara.

The audience went positively crazy. Each bear that came onstage seemed to get more laughs than the one before. Blaine Gibson had again turned Marc Davis's sketches into dimensional masterpieces of visual humor.

The Bears proved so popular that long lines became a permanent trade-

In 1986, the Country Bears premiered a new show that focused on their vacations across America (opposite, above, left). A scale model of "swingin'" Teddi Bara is fixed up for her act (right).

In 1974, Disneyland introduced its Bicentennial celebration with the patriotic musical revue America Sings, located in the former home of the Carousel of Progress in Tomorrowland (opposite, above, right). It was an extremely complicated show to program (below). The Bicentennial celebration continued with the spectacular America on Parade of 1975–76 (left).

When new Disney Chairman Michael Eisner first saw Disneyland, he thought it the "cleanest place on Earth" (opposite).

mark of the Country Bear Theater. The show seemed to be a natural addition for Disneyland, and the search began for a suitable location for a team of performing bears. One year later, in 1972, the attraction opened in twin theaters at Disneyland in the midst of a new land along the banks of the Rivers of America . . . Bear Country. It replaced the Indian Village above the banks of the Rivers of America, just above New Orleans Square.

MORE DISNEY CONTROVERSY

During his lifetime, Walt Disney received more than 960 major awards, including Oscars, television Emmies, gold records, the French Legion of Honor, and the Presidential Medal of Freedom. In 1973, the Disney family decided to create major showcases for the awards in both Disneyland and Walt Disney World. At the same time, WED completed a film that told the story of Walt's life, narrated by his own voice, taken from hundreds of tape-recorded interviews.

When "The Walt Disney Story" premiered in Florida, everything went smoothly. But at Disneyland, it was a whole different story. Noticing waning attendance at the Lincoln theater, Disney officials had decided to retire the Great Moments show and utilize the large theater for the new Disney film.

A public outcry followed, not about the arrival of Disney, but about the departure of Lincoln. Letters poured into the Disneyland office deploring the removal of "Walt Disney's greatest achievement and gift to America." Others suggested that the Disney organization had "succumbed to the same lack of patriotism that had already infected much of our nation."

So Mr. Lincoln came back for a return engagement. The original Great Moments show took the place of the film, and became the grand finale to the Walt Disney Story.

THE SOUNDS OF MUSIC

In 1973, shortly after Lincoln made his temporary departure, the Carousel of Progress made a permanent one, heading for Walt Disney World. General Electric felt its message had been delivered at Disneyland and wanted the chance to expose the show at the new Florida park.

One year later, riding a new swell of national patriotism, the first Disneyland "mega-musical," "America Sings," took its place. It used the same revolving carrousel facility, and featured a cast of 110 *Audio-Animatronics* char-

acters in an incredibly complex show. Its six different acts traced the development of musical styles across America, from gospel to country to rock 'n' roll. With its countless musical cues, moving scenery, and revolving theater, the attraction gave the WED designers more programming and timing problems than any other show.

For the nation's bicentennial celebration the following year, America Sings was joined by another musical burst of patriotism. "America on Parade" celebrated the country's people and accomplishments in a production that took years to mount. Dozens of parade floats were used to re-create famous scenes from American history, and the huge float that brought up the rear of the parade formed the largest American flag ever "flown." America on Parade joined a long tradition of live entertainment that has its own place in Disneyland history.

Millions of guests laughed at the antics at the Golden Horseshoe Revue in Frontierland, the longest-running production in show business annals . . . and gasped at the Fantasy in the Sky fireworks high over Sleeping Beauty Castle . . . and waved to the dancing characters during Fantasy on Parade . . . and marveled at the shimmering lights of the sparkling Electrical Parade . . . and thrilled to hundreds of rock bands, big bands, and marching bands . . . and celebrated the holidays, watching the Living Christmas Tree, Candlelight Procession, and the Christmas Parade. These, too, have become indispensable frames in the animated film called Disneyland.

Overleaf clockwise from above, left: *Fantasy in the Sky fireworks explode high above Sleeping Beauty Castle; Christmas at Disneyland is a glowing experience, especially as the annual Candlelight Procession passes the sixty-foot-tall Christmas tree in Town Square; Live entertainment at the Tomorrowland stage; The Main Street Electrical Parade, which harnesses millions of twinkling miniature lights, has been a traditional Disneyland favorite since its debut in 1972.*

The prefabricated peak of Big Thunder is hoisted by crane to the top of its steel structure. The mountain is constructed of steel and metal lathe, then coated with a thin shell of concrete. Mother Nature never imagined anything like this.

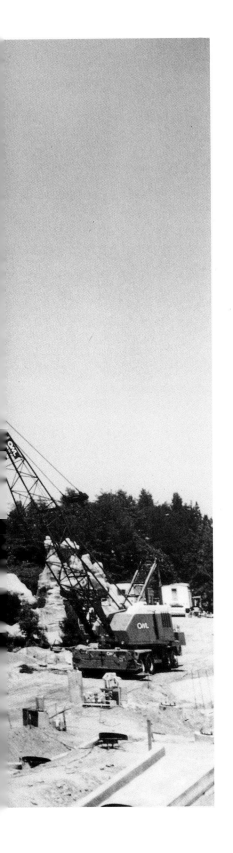

THE THRILLER ERA

Back in 1959, Matterhorn Mountain had become the first steel "thriller" ever produced. In earlier decades, roller coasters had been creaking and groaning with wooden construction, but the Swiss mountain at Disneyland changed all that. In its wake, a new era of thrillers known as "iron rides" swept across the nation. By the 1970s, these new thrillers had fueled an insatiable appetite in the "baby boomers," who were then moving rapidly into the entertainment marketplace.

At Disneyland, they surged to the Matterhorn, resulting in lines that seemed to go forever. In order to distribute the crowds, two more mountains began life on WED's drawing boards: a high-tech "Space Mountain" for Tomorrowland and "Big Thunder Mountain," whose southwest mesa and buttes towered over Frontierland. Sandwiched between the "mountain thrillers," in both time and space, was an extensive Matterhorn face lift and a renovation that added new scenes inside the mountain, an omnipresent Abominable Snowman, and, most important, doubled ride capacity.

Besides the obvious theme differences, each mountain offers its own unique features. Space Mountain is the first roller-coaster ride to occur in perpetual darkness. Its turbulent, twisting, special-effects-filled rocket journey through space is conducted in a universe housed totally inside the mountain. Not knowing where the turns and drops are coming from arouses a terrifying sense of fear and anticipation in the first-time "pilots."

Unlike the indoor Space Mountain, Big Thunder takes place mostly outdoors. For his first major project, designer Tony Baxter employed extensive animation and mechanical effects along the route of Big Thunder's "runaway" mine trains. He called into play flying bats, falling rocks, teetering buttes, earthquake effects (too realistic for some people), and splashdowns (too wet for others). It seems impossible for the first-time passenger to take it all in. "That's the whole point," says Baxter. "It's the same philosophy that Walt used on the Pirates. 'Give them more than they can see, and they'll keep coming back time and again.'"

Baxter belongs to the WED "baby boom," a new generation of Imagineers who understand, follow, and expand upon Walt Disney's design philosophies. Many of WED's "young lions" kept personal scrapbooks that they filled with childhood souvenirs of Disneyland.

For Tony Baxter, his next assignment was like a dream come true. He would soon go back to his childhood memories and remake them—the way they were supposed to be.

A runaway mine train careens into the town of Rainbow Ridge at the thrilling climax to "Big Thunder Mountain Railroad" (left). The scaled-down buildings that make up the town were originally built for the "Rainbow Caverns Mine Train" and have stood in Frontierland since 1956. In 1986, the Disneyland horses were brought from their back-stage Pony Farm to the onstage Big Thunder Ranch (above) for the enjoyment of the guests—and the horses themselves.

The actual loading area for Space Mountain (center) came very close to the artist's original concept (above). A year after Space Mountain opened, the Abominable Snowman, sculpted by Blaine Gibson, began to haunt the caverns of Matterhorn Mountain (below).

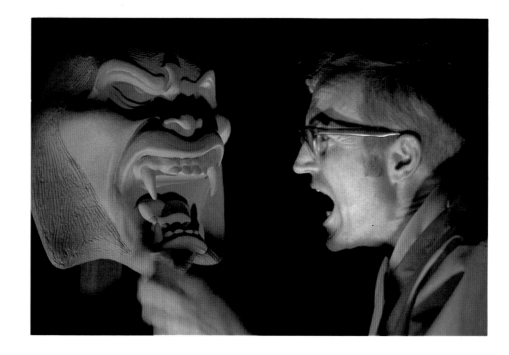

New Fantasyland is filled with the incredible make-believe architecture that time and money precluded in 1955.

This concept sketch depicts the new abode of Mr. Toad's Wild Ride, the zaniest attraction in new Fantasyland.

DREAMS REVISITED

For whatever reason, Walt never found the right time to do Fantasyland the way he really wanted to—not during the rush and budget-conscious period of getting Disneyland started, and not after the young park got on its feet. In 1983, the time finally came to create a proper home for the Disney characters whose mythology and stunning success had made the original Disneyland dream a reality.

In a way, the new Fantasyland forged a symbolic link between the pioneers and the inheritors of the Disneyland tradition. The team included Ken Anderson, the first Disney employee ever to work on Disneyland, and Tony Baxter, who as a child had vicariously lived every legend Anderson had helped to create.

With Anderson and Baxter's help, the Disney classic animated films took a giant step toward becoming a new and improved three-dimensional reality. The dark rides of the "New Fantasyland" explored the frightening world of Snow White, the escapism to "Never Land" by the child in all of us called Peter Pan, the moralistic fable of Pinocchio, the madcap, cacophonous fun of Mr. Toad, and, a short time later, the nonsensical world of Alice in Wonderland. All of the shows featured state-of-the-art effects, and, for the first time in Fantasyland, *Audio-Animatronics* figures.

The mechanisms of the glorious Dumbo attraction in new Fantasyland are plated with real gold—which will never tarnish.

Whenever Merlin visits Fantasyland, he selects a lucky youngster to pull the sword from the stone (below). *Whoever successfully meets the challenge of the Sword in the Stone rules over Fantasyland for the day. Guests spin their way through the Mad Tea Party in Fantasyland* (bottom).

Children Under Age 7
Must Be With
An Adult

Please, No Food,
Drinks Or Smoking

Color boards (below) *document and coordinate the incredible array of colors in the new Fantasyland. The boards are used as a guide by the artisans who paint the actual signs* (opposite), *scenery, and buildings.*

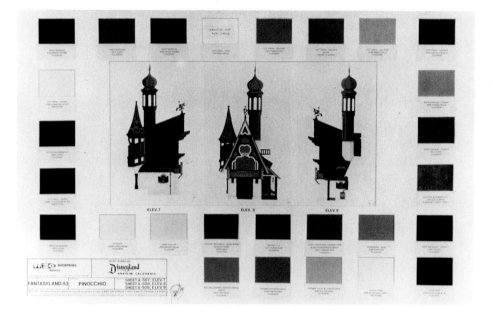

Overleaf, clockwise from above, left: *An artist works on one of the full-size murals for Pinocchio's Daring Journey, one of the totally new elements of the 1983 new Fantasyland; A concept sketch depicts the Frightening Forest in Snow White's Scary Adventures. The trees wait silently in the forest until the ride vehicles hurry by, and then their branches lunge out; "Off with their heads!" shouts the hot-headed Queen of Hearts, as guests invade her rose garden in Fantasyland's Alice in Wonderland; Peter Pan battles with Captain Hook in a new and more daring adventure in 1983; Flying high with Peter Pan over Never Land; Aboard Mr. Toad, the wildest ride in Fantasyland.*

Today, as one strolls through Fantasyland, accompanied by songs like "When You Wish upon a Star," where a wicked queen occasionally peers through just-parted curtains from a window above, where one is surrounded by wandering Disney characters and enveloped in charming architecture, slightly off center, just whimsical enough to have come only from someone's not-too-controlled dreams, one senses that now this place is the way it was meant to be. This is where the spirit of Disney would really want to reside.

JAWS

It was the spring of 1984. The Disney characters had barely snuggled into their new Fantasyland home when the storm clouds arrived—a storm that was, as they say in Hollywood, "years in the making." Disney films, with the exception of the animated features, were caught in a prolonged and deepening slump as movie audiences shunned G-rated productions in ever increasing numbers. After he replaced retiring Card Walker as Disney chief executive officer, Ron Miller had established a new film label, Touchstone, to produce pictures for a more mature audience without altering the Disney image.

But it was too late. The investment sharks of Wall Street smelled blood and moved in to attack. Corporate raider Saul Steinberg was the first to notice the slumping Disney stock. He began a hostile takeover bid that, if successful,

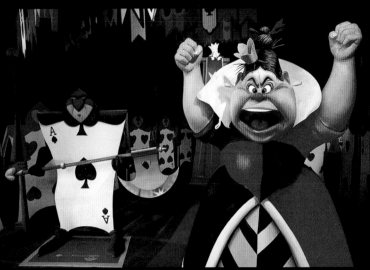

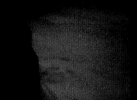

would have split apart the Disney company by selling its assets. Employing a defensive measure widely known as "greenmail," Disney bought back Steinberg's stock. The episode shook the entire Disney organization, along with the American public, which had naively viewed Mickey Mouse as sacred territory, not really subject to the tough realities of the business world.

The second attack came from another raider, Irwin Jacobs, who invested heavily in the now reeling Disney company and immediately began his own hostile bid. It was a traumatic time for everyone at Disney. A sense of gloom and total helplessness descended on the WED staff.

Ironically, this came at a time when WED was in the process of developing and implementing a long-range revitalization program designed to ensure that Disneyland would never fall victim to the same circumstances that were tormenting the film business. The first result of the strategy, begun a year earlier, was already in place, a brand-new *Circle-Vision* film, "American Journeys." It replaced the 1967 production of "America the Beautiful," which clearly showed its age with obsolete fashions, long-vanished skylines, and dated car styles.

While American Journeys played at Disneyland, the corporate drama played itself out at the Disney Studio. When the smoke cleared, Ron Miller was gone, the corporate sharks had left, the billionaire Bass brothers from Texas had become friendly major investors in the Disney organization, now called the Walt Disney Company, and Mickey and company got a new team to lead them to new horizons—Paramount President Michael Eisner joined with former Warner Bros. co-Chairman Frank Wells to become, respectively, chairman of the board and president, while Walt Disney's nephew Roy E. Disney assumed the role of vice-chairman of the board.

"IT'S BACK TO WORK WE GO"

Eisner and Wells faced the challenge of starting to rebuild the Studio before they could get around to WED. Eisner spent most of his waking hours "starting up" the new Studio team while Wells intensely studied everything imaginable about WED and the Disney theme parks. "We're back in show business again," Disney employees said with a sigh of relief. The comment soon proved to be an understatement. And, as a salute to the enduring spirit of the company's founder, WED Enterprises would soon be transformed into Walt Disney Imagineering.

The premiere of a new Country Bear show in Frontierland during the

Christmas holidays of 1984 marked the beginning of another strategy that had been established for revitalizing Disneyland. Earlier, WDI creative chief Marty Sklar had reviewed some rough sketches done by two young animation programmers. Each sketch took a specific *Audio-Animatronics* Country Bear performer and added new costumes, scenery, songs, and dialogue, all on the theme of Christmas. Could an existing facility and a familiar cast of characters be successfully transformed into an all-new show? The sketches said yes, and the show proved them right. "The Country Bear Christmas Special" became the hit of the 1984 holiday season. The WDI designers soon went back to the drawing boards to develop still another new show, "Country Bear Vacation Hoedown," which premiered in February 1986.

Another special enhancement came to a time-honored attraction located on Main Street, U.S.A. Using new technologies developed by scientists to maneuver artificial limbs, WDI animators rebuilt and completely reprogrammed the Abraham Lincoln figure. "It was kind of scary to see how realistic we could make him with the new technology," remembers WDI programmer Dave Feiten. "I couldn't resist pushing the animation movements as far as the new system would let me. I guess I sort of went too far. When I finished the program, we discovered that I had turned him into a hyperactive campaigning politician."

Feiten's next effort restored the dignity expected of a great president and created a performance light-years ahead of the "winkin' blinkin' Lincoln" of 1964. With new special effects, film, and music, the most realistic *Audio-Animatronics* figure in Disney history made Great Moments with Mr. Lincoln even greater.

THE GREAT VIDEOPOLIS RACE

While country bears and a famous president performed with new vitality, a great race began to clock off. The Tomorrowland stage, long a popular performance and dance area, had to be removed to make way for a project so secret that no one could talk about it. In its wake, the Park's live-entertainment producers, left frantically searching for a replacement dance area, descended on WDI to find a solution.

For three hectic days during the spring of 1985, Park representatives and WDI designers worked in near-desperation on a new facility concept and master plan. Only 105 days later, in a meadow area behind Fantasyland, Videopolis opened to the public. A live rock band played from a towering stage

In 1985, an unused area behind Fantasyland exploded to life and became the home of Videopolis, a huge outdoor nighttime dance club featuring state-of-the-art sound and video systems.

A technical check occurs before the new Circle-Vision *production,* American Journeys, *debuts* (below). *A new storage system enables Park projectionists to change shows rapidly during the day, making good use of the growing inventory of* Circle-Vision *productions made for other Disney theme parks.*
The original Country Bear show performs one last time before giving way to the new Vacation Hoedown (bottom).

structure that rose above thousands of guests dancing in a sprawling, open-air arena. Overhead, a giant grid structure slowly lowered from the ceiling, twisting and turning like a science-fiction space station as it sent a chorus line of pulsating searchlights into the sky. Throughout the area, camera crews captured the dancers in a live telecast, adding special electronics effects to produce a "real-time rock video" on a huge overhead screen.

"Videopolis gets three fs," mused WDI President Carl Bongirno on opening night. "The first, the fastest, and the finest—it is the first attraction completed under the new Eisner-Wells team; the fastest construction project we've ever completed; and the finest dance facility of its kind anywhere."

Meanwhile, in another part of town, word of the secret project was beginning to leak out. The world's reigning rock video superstar had joined forces with Disney.

CAPTAIN EO

Just before the Christmas holidays in 1984, WDI's Bongirno and Dick Nunis were discussing a call they had received from new Disney president Frank Wells. "What would your designers want to do if they could develop an attraction with Michael Jackson?" Wells had asked. Bongirno got an immediate response from his staff. Disney had developed the most sophisticated 3-D camera system in the world, a 70-millimeter system that had been used to create a stunning film for EPCOT Center in Walt Disney World. Starring Michael Jackson in a 70-millimeter, 3-D rock adventure at Disneyland seemed to be perfect casting.

Shortly after the holidays, WDI received its first visit from one of the Park's greatest fans. Accompanied by Jeffrey Katzenberg, the head of Walt Disney Pictures, Michael Jackson met with the WDI design staff and listened to the 3-D film proposal. "I think it's a really great idea," he observed, "but I'd like to do it with George or Steven." Everyone around the table recognized the Hollywood shorthand for George Lucas and Steven Spielberg. Lucas had already been working with WDI on several ideas that might bring his *Star Wars* mythology to Tomorrowland. The timing seemed opportune.

WDI designer Rick Rothschild headed up a concept team that sketched out three different screen scenarios for Jackson and Lucas to consider at the next meeting. They both picked the same story—Jackson would play a space pilot named Captain Eo, whose mission was to bring music and dance to a distant planet to break the spell of a wicked queen.

Produced by Lucas and directed by Francis Ford Coppola, the production brought together an impressive array of creative talent from around the entertainment industry. Yet the show would not be limited to the screen. "While the film was being produced on one side of town," says WDI's Rothschild, "we had to create a theater that was so laden with special effects that the audience would feel that they had been drawn right into the movie."

Rothschild's team created smoke effects that would roll into the theater when Jackson's spaceship crashed. They built a fiber-optic star field that enhanced and extended the film's own galaxy beyond the screen's dimensions. They installed laser units behind the screen that would fire over the audience's heads during the battle sequences. "We wound up with more than 150 special effects in the show," Rothschild said. "But producing the effects was the easy part. Getting them to coordinate precisely with the effects on the film nearly drove us crazy."

The project nearly drove everybody else crazy, too. Schedules slipped, budgets drained, marketing plans changed, and frustrations flourished. In other words, it was just like any other Disneyland project.

The opening night of "Captain Eo," however, was quite unlike any other in the long and storied past of Disneyland. It set off a party that kept the Park open for sixty straight hours—a genuine Hollywood-style premiere, which, through the Eisner/Katzenberg film connections, brought out more entertainment celebrities than at any other time since the Park's grand opening more than three decades earlier.

GEORGE LUCAS: TAKE TWO

For several years, WDI designers had toyed with the idea of using flight simulator technology as a basis for a new kind of attraction. Imagineers booked rides on all kinds of simulators that trained pilots for helicopters, giant passenger planes, and jet fighters. A simulator motion base looks like a giant table top, with hydraulic pistons for legs. As the pistons move up and down, the platform tilts and twists like a robotic bucking bronco, faithfully re-creating almost any motion encountered in a flight situation.

When George Lucas began working with WDI on new attractions for Tomorrowland, the simulator was clearly an idea whose time had come. The notion of taking the spectacular high-action scenes of *Star Wars* and projecting them in a theater that could twist and shake, producing real aerial combat sensations, excited everyone, including Lucas himself.

Michael Jackson arrived at Tomorrowland in September 1986 in the person of Captain Eo, star of a spectacular 3-D space adventure produced by George Lucas and directed by Francis Coppola (opposite and above, left).

A Disney Imagineer checks REX to make sure he's fit for flight aboard Star Tours (above, right). Disney Chairman Michael Eisner and producer George Lucas oversee the dedication of Star Tours in January 1987 (below).

"When we started discussing the idea," says WDI's Tony Baxter, "George immediately saw the potential. But he wanted to put a new twist on the story. Disneyland had always been known as the place where nothing could go wrong. In this show something *would* go wrong."

Lucas and WDI show producer Tom Fitzgerald worked out a story line for "Star Tours," an intergalactic sightseeing company that would whisk guests around the universe in all the comfort of a luxury jetliner. "George wanted to make the audience think the spaceship was a typical Disneyland ride vehicle on a track," says Fitzgerald. (The designers programmed vibrations and bumps into the motion base to make the passengers believe they were actually moving along a track.) "Then, look out! Something really does go wrong. Although we saw the ship ahead of us successfully blast off on its mission, we take a wrong turn, blunder through the maintenance doors, and start Disneyland's first 'misadventure.'" Causing the misadventure in the first place is a friendly but totally incompetent droid pilot named Rex, whose presence in the flight cabin brings a humorous Lucas touch to the journey.

As the Star Tours project rambled along toward its January 1987 premiere, few Imagineers doubted that WDI was producing perhaps its most exciting new adventure since Pirates of the Caribbean. The simulator test facility on WDI's lot had run dozens of test shows that had thrilled and stunned employees and their families, usually a tough, sophisticated audience much more difficult to impress than the public at large. When the time for the show's grand opening at Disneyland arrived, it was a foregone conclusion that Star Tours would be a "home run." Actually, it was a "grand slam home run," ushered in by another, even grander Hollywood-style premiere and another sixty-hour party.

NEW HORIZONS

"The way I see it," Walt Disney often said, "Disneyland will never be finished. It's something we can keep developing and adding to." His comments seem to have made an indelible impression on the organization Walt Disney left behind. In the more than two decades since his passing, not only did Disneyland continue to grow and flourish, but the theme park also moved to Florida in the form of Walt Disney World's Magic Kingdom, traveled across the Pacific Ocean as a Tokyo Disneyland, and went back to Florida with

A Star Tours mural adorns a corridor of Tomorrowland (opposite).

the creation of EPCOT Center. Today, with four major theme parks in operation and another on the horizon in Europe, one might assume that Disneyland, the original, could be somewhat overshadowed in the future.

"Not so," says Disney's Michael Eisner. "Disneyland remains the flagship," he maintains, "the experimental place to do things that could translate to our other parks. To keep Disneyland on the leading edge, we'll be constantly looking at new ways to combine art and technology, just as Disney has always done. But the main emphasis will remain—that we're there to entertain and be creative and fanciful, while we look to the brighter side of things."

Looking to the brighter side of things has certainly been the trademark of Disneyland since its very beginning. "When you react to things, you're alive," says John Hench, reflecting on his half-century career at Disney. "I think people in Disneyland react and expand very easily. Unlike in society's modern cities, they can drop their defenses in Disneyland and look other people in the eye. Actually, what we're selling throughout the Park is reassurance. We offer adventures in which you survive a kind of personal challenge—a charging hippo, a runaway mine train, a wicked witch, an out-of-control bobsled. But in every case, we let you win. We let your survival instincts triumph over adversity. A trip to Disneyland is an exercise in reassurance about oneself and one's ability to maybe even handle the real challenges in life."

Designer Tony Baxter speaks for the new WDI generation that grew up on the reassurance that Hench helped to create. "I don't ever ask myself if Walt would like this or that," he says. "Most of us today have been around Disney since we were kids. If we don't have a feeling for what it means now, we wouldn't be here. When we work on a project, we really have everybody put their feelings into it. That's our best assurance for future success."

Today Baxter is putting his feelings into a new attraction for Disneyland. "Splash Mountain" is the assignment—a twisting, plummeting water-thrill adventure that combines the best of a flume ride and Disney place-making mythos. Based on the classic feature *Song of the South*, it will incorporate Brer Bear, Brer Fox, and Brer Rabbit into an adventure that is as classically Disney as Disneyland itself.

For the grand opening, scheduled for early 1989, there might even be another sixty-hour party. Most important, though, for those who have followed Disneyland since its inception, Splash Mountain will be one more in the continuing flow of new ideas designed to preserve and extend Walt Disney's dream—a simple dream for a place "where parents and children can have fun together."

Disneyland chief designer Tony Baxter and show designer Chris Tietz (above) *put the final details on the scale model of Splash Mountain* (below). *The giant waterfall drop will be the highest in the world, plunging guests more than fifty-two feet into the river below. Splash Mountain premieres at Disneyland in 1989.*

APPENDIX

Sequence of
Disneyland Attractions

Note: Numbers refer to pages; numbers in *italics* refer to illustrations.

Attraction	Opening Date
King Arthur Carrousel	July 1955
6, 80–81, *82*	
Peter Pan Flight (later renamed **Peter Pan's Flight**)	July 1955
81, *83*, 86	
Mad Tea Party	July 1955
223	
Mr. Toad's Wild Ride	July 1955
81, 86	
Canal Boats of the World	July 1955
116–17, 128	
Snow White's Adventures	July 1955
81, 86	
Tomorrowland Autopia	July 1955
88–89, *90*, 97, 143, 148, 204	
Space Station X-1 (later renamed **Satellite View of America**)	July 1955
88	
Disneyland Railroad	July 1955
64, *64*, 185	
Circarama	July 1955
89, 143	
Horse-Drawn Street Cars	July 1955
2, *22*, *84–85*, 122	
Horse-Drawn Fire Wagon	July 1955
Main Street Cinema	July 1955
Horse-Drawn Surreys	July 1955
Jungle Cruise	July 1955
24, 68, 69, *70*, 71–73, *72*, 112, 115, 157, *158–59*, 160–61, *161*	
Stage Coach	July 1955
76, 119–20, *120–21*, 122	
Mule Pack (later renamed **Pack Mules**)	July 1955
76	
Mark Twain Steamboat	July 1955
1, 64, 76, *76*, 77, *78–79*, 93, 97, 104–105, *105*, 115, 128, *130*	
Main Street Penny Arcade	July 1955
2, 60	
Golden Horseshoe Revue	July 1955
76, 79, 93, 213	
Indian Village, near **Adventureland**	July 1955
Hall of Chemistry	July 1955
143, *184*, 185, *185*	
Rocket to the Moon	July 1955
88, *141*, 143	
Main Street Shooting Gallery	July 1955
Phantom Boats	July 1955
119, *120*	
Casey Jr. Circus Train	July 1955
81, *83*	
Color Gallery	Summer 1955
143	
The World Beneath Us	Summer 1955
88	
Davy Crockett Museum	Summer 1955
Dairy Bar	Summer 1955

Attraction	Opening Date
20,000 Leagues Under the Sea	August 1955
91, 91–92, 143	
Dumbo Flying Elephants	August 1955
83	
Conestoga Wagons	August 1955
76	
Mickey Mouse Club Theater	August 1955
Thimble Drome Flight Circle (later renamed **Tomorrowland Flight Circle**) *141*, 143	September 1955
Mickey Mouse Club Circus	November 1955
124–25, *125*	
Mike Fink Keel Boats	December 1955
128, *129*	
Hall of Aluminum Fame	December 1955
143	
Astro-Jets	March 1956
201	
Bathroom of Tomorrow	April 1956
Horseless Carriage (Red)	May 1956
64	
Storybook Land Canal Boats	June 1956
117, *118–19*, 119	
Tom Sawyer Island Rafts	June 1956
27, *106*, 208	
Skyway to Tomorrowland	June 1956
128, *134–35*, *142*, 204	
Skyway to Fantasyland	June 1956
125, *126*	
Rainbow Ridge Pack Mules	June 1956
122, *122–123*	
Rainbow Mountain Stage Coach	June 1956
Rainbow Caverns Mine Train	July 1956
129, *131*, 132, 161, *218*	
Indian Village, near **Frontierland**	July 1956
129, *130*	
Indian War Canoes	July 1956
128, *130–31*	
Junior Autopia	July 1956
Main Street Omnibus #1	August 1956
Horseless Carriage (Yellow)	December 1956
64	
Midget Autopia	April 1957
Sleeping Beauty Castle Walk-Through	April 1957
140	
Holidayland	June 1957
House of the Future	June 1957
Viewliner	June 1957
143–45, *144*	
Motor Boat Cruise	June 1957
Indian Village Rafts	July 1957
Frontierland Shooting Gallery	July 1957
Main Street Omnibus #2	December 1957
Grand Canyon Diorama	March 1958
138, 140–41, 185	
Alice in Wonderland	June 1958